PENPRENEUR

No AI Gimmicks.
No Kindle Publishing.
No Freelancing or Copywriting.

Just <u>Pen</u>, <u>Paper</u> & Your <u>Brain</u>!

PENPRENEUR

HOW TO MAKE SIX FIGURES WRITING ONE THING A MONTH

SCOTT P. SCHEPER

Greenlamp
CALIFORNIA

For Your Bibcard:

Scheper, Scott. *Penpreneur: How to Make Six Figures Writing One Thing a Month*. California: Greenlamp Publishing, 2024.

Copyright © 2024 by Scheper Research, LLC. All rights not not reserved.

No portion of this book may be reproduced in any format without written permission from the author.

Published in the United States of America by Greenlamp Publishing, an imprint of Greenlamp LLC, Orange County, California.

Greenlamp Publishing
30021 Tomas, Suite 300
Rancho Santa Margarita, CA 92688

ISBN: 978-1-963977-10-3

Legal Disclaimer

The term *entrepreneur* is of French origin. *Entre* means "under," and *preneur* means "to take." An *entrepreneur* is an "undertaker" of risk. As an entrepreneur, you are undertaking a journey at your own risk. There is no guarantee the methods outlined in this book will result in success for you. Your success depends on many factors—your effort, your persistence, your previous knowledge (and other variables). While every attempt has been made to verify the data in this book, you are responsible for your own success.

AI Disclaimer

0% of this book was created using AI. This book was written out by hand on 4x6" notecards. It was then typed out and edited by its author. Then, it was printed and redlined using a Montblanc pen with Modena red ink. It was finally edited once more and sent off to a typesetter.

Dedication

I dedicate this book to my wife, the love of my life. Thank you for believing in me (despite the fact that when you met me, I was a 37-year-old who was down on his luck, living with his parents). This book shares the business model that turned my life around.

Special Acknowledgment

I would like to express my gratitude to Sam Markowitz. Sam is a marketing genius who originally got his start as the last protégé of the late Gary Halbert, a man who is widely considered the greatest direct response marketer of all time.

Sam operates "behind the scenes" of many businesses. He is responsible for more business successes than you can count. When a business isn't merely looking for growth, but is <u>specifically</u> seeking "hyper-growth," they come to Sam.

Sam is also one of the kindest people I know, and I am truly blessed to call him a mentor. I am honored to have him write the foreword to this book.

Thank you, Sam, for changing my life.

Contents

Foreword 13
Preface 17

{ Part 1 } Trapped

Chapter One / Disenchanted 35
Chapter Two / Wants 39
Chapter Three / Desires 41
Chapter Four / False Paths 53
Chapter Five / The Spark 59
Chapter Six / Doubts 65

{ Part 2 } Decisions

Chapter Seven / Ignoring The Mormon 73
Chapter Eight / The Digital Publishing Journey 75
Chapter Nine / The Launch 79
Chapter Ten / The Return of the Mormon! 85
Chapter Eleven / A New Hope 91

{ Part 3 } Trials

Chapter Twelve / The Hidden Power of Analog 97
Chapter Thirteen / The Hidden Power of Knowledge 103
Chapter Fourteen / The Final Hidden Power 109
Chapter Fifteen / Analog Publishing Revolution 117
Chapter Sixteen / The One Funnel to Rule Them All 123

{ Part 4 } Action

Chapter Seventeen / The Teeniest, Tiniest Niche Ever?..... 133
Chapter Eighteen / No Thanks, Hawaii 141
Chapter Nineteen / Engulfed by a Bear........................ 147
Chapter Twenty / Finally... 153

{ Part 5 } Rebirth

Chapter Twenty-One / To Teach, or Not To Teach........... 161
Chapter Twenty-Two / Push-Button Simple................... 175
Chapter Twenty-Three / Freedom Writers..................... 179
Chapter Twenty-Four / The Crazy Ones 189
Chapter Twenty-Five / A Look Back............................ 193
Chapter Twenty-Six / Tribe of Superfans..................... 197
Chapter Twenty-Seven / A Look Ahead 201

Appendix A / Penpreneur Creed................................. 205

Glossary... 215
Selected Bibliography 219
Index... 223
About the Author.. 225
Greenlamp 227

Foreword

From the Desk Of:
Sam Markowitz
Thursday, 11:53 a.m.
Tel Aviv, Israel

You are about to embark on a fascinating journey that can greatly impact your life.

In *Penpreneur*, Scott Scheper shares how he discovered a unique business model that finally brought him everything he has always desired in life.

He shares how he started off dead broke, working a job he hated...

He searches out many different ways of working for himself, experiencing a long series of failures...

He eventually makes millions of dollars, but realizes it came at the cost of him turning into a workaholic. He became a slave to his business and even ended up getting divorced...

He then leaves that business and finally discovers a business model that gives him all the money he could ever ask for—as well as a lifestyle filled with freedom and joy.

Scott shares this journey through a series of stories, lessons, and "aha" moments that all sequentially unravel the principles behind the *Penpreneur* lifestyle.

You will discover how he's been able to pursue a passion of his—in an extremely tiny niche—and how he built an audience of just a few thousand people that makes him well over six figures a year—all while working just a few hours a month. Scott then shares how this business model serves as the foundation for scaling to seven figures a year.

What brings Scott the most fulfillment is knowing he is making a positive impact on thousands of people's lives.

Scott takes a "non-traditional" approach to what most people do. It is usually through doing something different that breakthroughs occur. It is precisely the uniqueness of his approach that makes this lifestyle business so successful.

This book shares what he is doing, and it is

easily replicable by anyone who wishes to do the same.

Scott could have kept this unique business model to himself. But when he realized there were so many others like him who could benefit tremendously from it, he decided to share it.

Today, he enjoys helping many others pursue their passions—and that's why he wrote this book.

Get ready to have a whole new world opened up to you in the following pages.

Sincerely,

Samuel Markowitz

Sam Markowitz
SamMarkowitzGroup.com

Preface

From:
Scott P. Scheper
Rancho Santa Margarita, Calif.
Thursday, 2:48 p.m.

Dear Friend,

What you have in your hands is a book that took me sixteen years to write. After you finish it, you will save yourself sixteen years of learning things the <u>expensive</u> way, which is...

Learning Through Experience!

I was faced with several decisions when I set out to write this book. First, I noticed a trend among business authors wherein they "brain dump" everything into a book. They enthrall you with diagrams of "frameworks." They give you exhaustive mental models and strategies, and—by the end of the book—you don't know where to even begin!

Initially, I was planning on going this route. However, I realized that giving you "everything there is to know" would <u>not</u> be of service to you. Instead, I decided to cut all the fat. That's right. I decided to focus on giving you...

**The Only
Thing You Need
to Know!**

By the end of this book, you will have a three-word answer to the question, "How do you make six figures writing one thing a month?"

After you finish this book, you will understand <u>the</u> most powerful business model for independent writers, researchers, and entrepreneurs. It is <u>the</u> <u>only</u> thing you need to know!

Whether you desire to be an independent writer, or—if you're a coach, consultant, or course creator looking to skyrocket your growth (to $100,000 per month and beyond)—then guess what? You don't need to focus on anything else other than what you're about to learn in this book.

Writing the book with this goal in mind was the first decision I made.

The second decision I made concerned how I would go about teaching you this business model. I thought about it, and soon the answer became clear. I recalled a quote by Ernest Hemingway...

**"The Writer's Job Is
to Tell The Truth."**

I could have painted this business model as a simple journey, but—the *truth* is... it took me many years to get right! If I merely taught you the concepts without any background context, it wouldn't have a lasting impact on your life.

Therefore, I decided to unpack each concept by sharing my entire journey. By teaching you this business model through detailing my actual true journey, you will remember it much longer. You will also better understand why each component in this business model works so well. You will see how doing things differently than what I now prescribe resulted in painful failures for me. Knowing these specific details will save you time and money. You will have already learned from my failures. Overall, the idea is...

**Through My Story,
You Will Better Retain These Lessons
For The Rest of Your Life!**

When I write about specific moments where I found myself stuck, chances are you've been in a similar position. Even if you haven't, there's a chance you will someday. In such cases, my journey will serve as a guide for helping you get "unstuck."

The main point is—this book was written <u>very</u> intentionally. You may not realize it, but—down the road—when you encounter difficult challenges in your business (or life), you're going to think back to something you read about in this book. It will help guide you through <u>anything</u> that arises in the future.

Now—before moving any further—as you've probably noticed, I write in a peculiar way. I use an old-school typewriter font. I also leverage a technique called...

"Subheads"

Subheads are center-aligned headlines. They were used by copywriters from the "pre-internet days." Adding subheads creates "eye relief" for readers. It also keeps readers in a state of *momentum*.

Truthfully, I use such techniques not for your pleasure but as an *homage* to the greatest copywriter who ever lived, Gary C. Halbert.

Halbert's style has inspired my own, and through my voice, I hope you can hear echoes of his.

I write in a way that "simplifies" concepts by making use of quotations for emphasis. I opt for a light-hearted tone, instead of pedantic and academic. This style is not typically used by modern business authors. The reason why is because I believe such authors aren't truly <u>free</u>. They're puppets who must pander to publishing houses and pleat-pantsed editors.

Even so, I want you to understand—although I write in this way (and make liberal use of ellipses and exclamations), the material you will find in this book is to be taken <u>very</u> seriously. In the following pages, I'll be introducing you to **a business model that is <u>powerful</u> yet deceptively <u>simple</u>.**

I will be sharing my successes (and failures) in discovering this business model. By illustrating my experiences, I hope to get one thing across to you:

Test What I Say!

That's right, **<u>test</u>** what I say. I want you to take what I teach you in this book and try it for yourself—**<u>exactly</u>** as I've laid out. <u>Do</u>

not read what I say and add your own "spin" to things. The rule I want you to follow is...

First Imitate, Then Innovate!

Listen: There's a rule I have people write down on a notecard whenever I begin working with them. The rule is, **"Do what Scott says!"**

I cannot tell you how many times I've seen people fail because they, (a) listened to what I taught them, and then (b) immediately added their own spin to things. **In reality, adding your own "spin" is just your mind tricking you into cutting corners.**[1]

The reason this book is going to have such a lasting impact on your life is because you'll understand **how** and **why** it all came to be.

I've written the book in such a way that the chapters are bite-sized. I did this because I don't want you to get stuck. I want you to stay

---

1 For instance, one year ago, I taught someone the business model you're about to learn in this book. This person was an experienced marketer. He had twenty years of experience under his belt. After hearing what I had to say, he went and did the exact opposite. He created a digital monthly newsletter and charged $10/month. He thought he was "adding his own spin" to things. Fast forward to today, and guess what? He folded that venture because (surprise, surprise) it didn't work. He experienced one year of learning things the expensive way. This is but one example. I have many others. The lesson? First imitate, then innovate. Do exactly as I say.

in a state of momentum. I want you to finish the book. After you do, you will have a business model imprinted on your mind for the rest of your life. **I hold that this business model is the <u>best</u> foundation for <u>any</u> type of *knowledge business* out there** (writing, coaching, consulting, education, courses, and more).

Recently, Dan Kennedy, a renowned author and copywriter, sold his business. I was listening to an interview with its new owner.[2] At the center of Kennedy's business is the model you're about to learn about in this book. Kennedy described it as the "tent pole" of a massive festival tent. At the center is "the tent pole around which everything else you do with your customers revolves," Kennedy says.[3] The very best businesses are like giant festivals—where you invite people in so that they can invest in everything else.

This book teaches you how to build the tent pole. After you build it, your festival will be filled with your fans who are excited to invest in your other products and services.

---

[2] Russell Brunson Talks Building ClickFunnels to $200M a Year, Struggles, & The Future of Marketing, 2024. Ryan Pineda, 58:11.

[3] Dan Kennedy, "A Lesson I Still Use From My 'Amway' Days...," Magnetic Marketing Blog.

Which brings me to...

Who This Book Is For

This book is for two types of people:

1) Independent Writers, Creators, and Researchers

This book is for you if you want to spend your days in peace. It's for the <u>introverts</u> at heart. If you want to spend your days reading, writing, and thinking—<u>without</u> having to "hustle" for clients—then this book will be life-changing.

What you will learn in this book is the business model that unlocks what you've always desired—*the neo-intellectual life* (which I'll define later).

This book is equally for...

2) Entrepreneurs, Coaches, Consultants, and Course Creators

If you don't see yourself as a "writer," this book is still for you. However—and here's the key—it's only for you if you're open to the idea that packaging your knowledge in a specific way will transform your entire business (and life).

What you will learn in this book will become the rock upon which your church is built.

Instead of having to look for new clients every month, you'll have a loyal tribe of superfans—people who already *know* you, *like* you, and *trust* you—people who will be emailing you, asking to work with you—<u>every single day</u>!

Instead of struggling to sell courses, consulting, or coaching, you'll have a *recurring* stream of new customers ready to purchase your high-ticket offers on demand.

No longer will you have to go out searching for clients. Your clients will <u>already</u> be in your festival tent! They'll be begging to work with you!

If you are a coach, consultant, or any other type of service provider, you have an advantage. Your advantage is that you probably have a high-value offering. (i.e., a high-priced product or service.) You see, by pairing your high-value offering with the business model you're about to learn in this book, you can scale your business to seven figures and beyond—in a relatively short amount of time, too!

For many people, just making six figures writing one thing a month is enough. For those who want more, the path is the same. Getting to six figures with this model is the <u>precursor</u> to seven figures. Therefore, for our purposes, we're going to focus on the first objective—getting to six figures writing one thing a month.

When I refer to you as an "independent writer, creator, and researcher," I'm also referring to entrepreneurs, coaches, consultants—and, honestly—**<u>anyone</u> who wants to package their knowledge into a *written asset***. That is, a *written asset* that generates recurring wealth for the rest of your life.

While there are ways of implementing this model without writing anything yourself, I do not recommend it. After sixteen years of trying (and failing), **I've found that it's best to only do things you <u>truly</u> believe in.** It may seem counterintuitive, but...

The Slow Way, The Hard Way, The Deliberate Way— Is The Best Way.

This is why I recommend first writing things out by hand. This very idea—this paragraph, this sentence—the words you are reading right now—they are being written out by hand—in ink—right now in front of my face.

In the time it took me to write that previous paragraph, I could have typed out five paragraphs and diarrhea'd a bunch of ChatGPT onto this page, but I didn't. Why? Because that is what losers do. Seriously. That is the road of shortcuts. Shortcuts lead to creating work that you will not be proud of.

I have a folder on my computer containing fifty ventures I've launched in the past. However, I quit them all. Why? **Because they were money-driven, not heart-driven.** The game we're playing is one in which we must move slowly. We must create an asset that lasts ten, twenty, thirty, or hell—even a hundred years after we die! Books have such longevity. That is the game we're playing. A game where we're creating a body of work that we can stand behind. Something "built to last."

You have stumbled not into a new business model, but a new philosophy. As such, a better question to ask is...

Who Is This Book NOT For?

This book is not for two groups of people:

1) Make-Money Online Bros

If you like jumping from one shiny object to

to the next, this book is not for you. This is not for the "make money online" crowd. For instance, the twenty-year-old internet marketing bro who—every other month—shifts between eCommerce, AI, crypto, TikTok, drop-shipping, and whatever else is "hot" right now.

This book is for those who are willing to focus on one thing.

Which brings me to the second type of person this book is not for...

2) Those Who Do Not Care About The Craft of Writing

If you're the type who wants to publish a ton of crap on Kindle for "passive income" (which, by the way, is a lie)—then this book is not for you.

I'm serious. At the time I'm writing this, there's a group of goons out there who are gaining a lot of popularity. They're hyping the (old) idea that you can make "passive income" by publishing on Amazon. In reality, they themselves don't publish on Amazon! (They make their money selling *courses,* not selling on Amazon themselves.) These goons proffer advice such as, "Your book should *not* be new information." They say, "Your job is to take good information on your topic that is scattered on the internet... and organize it in a book."[4]

If publishing gibberish is something you'd like to do, this book is <u>not</u> for you.

You'll find people who <u>do</u> make money pursuing activities <u>solely</u> for money's sake—but ultimately—it's a mirage! (And I have the scars to prove it!) If you're only after "fast money," you're looking at a world of hurt. You're looking at burnout, lawsuits, and nights asking yourself, "Why did I get into this in the first place?"

Do things the <u>right way</u>, the <u>slow way</u>, the <u>deliberate way</u>—and I promise you—it will pay off in the end.

Yes, there will still be trials and tribulations. There will be doubts—days when you ask yourself, "Why am I working so hard and making so little?" But I promise you—if you **press on**, slowly and deliberately, you will get to the promised land. This book is going to give you the only business model you need for the rest of your life.

---

4   Mikkelsen Twins, *The Freedom Shortcut*. (Publishing Life, 2021), 151.

Get ready,
And always remember,
To stay crispy, my friend.

Scott P. Scheper

"A Man Who is Honored to Be of Service to You"

P.S. Here's how I recommend you read this book: (1) Read this entire book <u>without</u> taking any notes. Do not get distracted. Don't Google any footnotes. Stay focused. Just read. (2) After you finish the book, write down <u>one</u> *irresistible* idea. Do this by listing the page number and the irresistible idea on a vertical 4x6" notecard (known as a "bibcard"). Trust that you'll remember the irresistible idea after you finish the book. Don't get bogged down by taking notes. Just read!

P.S. #2: It may help to purchase a "cube timer." (Just search "cube timer" on *Amazon*.) Purchase one with a label on the side that reads "60 minutes." Read in 60-minute increments. You'll finish in no time.

{ Part I }
Trapped

Chapter One

Disenchanted

It all began sixteen years ago. I was in my early twenties working at a technology startup. My job title was "Growth Hacker."[1] Ten-hour workdays were the norm. Working weekends was rewarded. It was a fast-paced "hustle culture" environment. It was fun—for a while. But soon, I became—let's just call it... **"disenchanted."**

It didn't matter that I was disenchanted. I had no other choice but to work. I was dead broke. I had just invested everything I had into a town house. Which meant, I now had a mortgage payment.[2] Which meant, I couldn't afford to quit my job. Which meant, I had to

---

1 A term popularized by a marketer named Sean Ellis. Frankly, I find the term rather banal.

2 At the root of mortgage is the Latin term, "mortem," which means death. The lesson? The only way out of a mortgage is death. (Remember this before you take on any debt.)

keep working at the tech startup—the job I hated.

   I was newly married to my first wife (aka, "tryout spouse"). Working nights and weekends on a side project wasn't an option. Why? Because I felt bad coming home after a full day of work, then heading upstairs and working in my home office (while my tryout spouse watched Netflix alone). That's right, I felt bad about doing that. Working in the same room with her while she watched Netflix wasn't an option. You see, I'm ADHD and—in order to work—I need to be in a _quiet_ environment. Zero distractions. I simply cannot drown out external noise while working.

   Working in the mornings wasn't the best option either. At the time, I was living in Irvine, California. The company I worked for was located one hour away in a beach town called Carlsbad. I was on the road for one hour in the morning and one hour in the evening. Basically, I was on the road for two hours every day! As a result, my days were cut short.

   The way I saw it was...

I Was Trapped!

   I was trapped in a job I hated and there was no viable way of getting out. I _did_ believe there were other viable "business models" out there. However, from what I saw—many of those business models consisted of "infoproduct gurus" teaching courses on how to make money online. I didn't want to create marketing courses. I wanted to simply read, think, and write.

Because my time was limited, I needed a **strategy**—the <u>right</u> strategy. That is, I needed to work smarter, not harder.

While I knew having the right strategy was important, I also knew I needed **accountability**. I needed a **mentor**. I needed a person who was <u>already</u> <u>having</u> <u>success</u>, and—just as important—someone who could hold me accountable.

Why did I need accountability? Because I had other important obligations in my life. For instance, I was the caretaker of my grandpa on the weekends. He wasn't doing well, and I spent my weekends taking care of him. Without someone holding <u>me</u> accountable, I knew I wouldn't want to work on a "side hustle" after spending the day taking care of my grandpa.

In brief, I needed the <u>correct</u> strategy—and, I also needed someone to kick me in the ass to keep me in a state of <u>momentum</u>!

This was the predicament in which I found myself when I started this journey. I'm guessing you may have found yourself in a similar situation.

At that point, I knew what I <u>didn't</u> want, but it's more important to get clear on what you <u>do</u> want. This is what we'll explore in the next chapter.

Chapter Two

Wants

What I wanted was a job I didn't hate. (I also didn't want to be on the road for two hours a day.)

Yet, deep down, I wanted to do something more <u>fulfilling</u> but—here's the catch...

**I Wanted to Do Something That
Would Also Pay The Mortgage!**

At the time, my mortgage was $2,600 and I could barely afford it. Ultimately, I wanted something that could grow to $10,000 per month in profit. Why? Because I was really after one thing...

Freedom!

I wanted more freedom in order to spend time with my spouse and my family. However, there was one condition: I didn't want to be stressed from work when I got home! I wanted to be fully present. I didn't want a life like the one I was living.

At that time, whenever I was not at work, I felt the urge to constantly check my company's *Slack* channel.[1] I was constantly on the lookout for anything urgent, even on the weekends. Instead of this, I wanted a life centered around freedom.

An important step preceding any major change is gaining clarity on your "wants." However, deep down within all of us is a calling—a purpose. You can solve for your **external** wants, but if you do not address your **internal** desires, then you will be stuck in an unfulfilled recurring loop for the rest of your life.

Gaining clarity on your *internal* desires is what we'll cover next.

---

[1] At that time, we actually used Skype, but you get the point.

Chapter Three

Desires

True... I wanted a job I didn't hate. Yet, deep down, I desired something more.

As I said, I was currently working at my first "real" job. Prior to that, I had graduated from college where I had gone through a major personal transformation. It's important you understand this, which is why I'm going to detail it now...

You see, in first grade, I was diagnosed with ADHD. School never held my attention. Due to my preference for "dicking around" in class, I was frequently reprimanded by teachers. I was labeled a "class clown." I was put into an improvement program for those who were "ungifted."

As a result of this, I had adopted an identity of being "ungifted." For the first eighteen years of my life, I truly believed I was dumb. As a result, I didn't bother trying in school. Why would I? I was "ungifted." I might as well focus on the things I *was* good at. (As you can probably guess, with this attitude, I got poor grades.)

Even though I never read the books I was assigned, I always loved reading. A teacher would assign me a chapter of *A Tale of Two Cities* by Charles Dickens. I'd go home and read all night—except, I'd read the *Redwall* series by Brian Jacques.

Despite *never* doing homework, I tested well on standardized tests and got admitted into a small private university in Southern California called *Chapman University*.

I remember the day like yesterday. In one of my high school classes, there was a wall in which the teacher pinned acceptance letters from universities. Every Friday, the teacher would ask if anyone had a new acceptance letter. A student would raise their hand and give the teacher the acceptance letter. We were all told to clap and cheer them on.

On Friday, the teacher asked for acceptance letters. I raised my hand. "Where were you accepted from, Scott?" I told the teacher I had been accepted into Chapman University. She was incredulous. "Do you have the letter?" she asked. "No," I said. "I was notified online." She smirked.

The following Monday, I came in with the acceptance letter. She looked shocked. She begrudgingly pinned it to the wall. I beat the system, I thought to myself.

Somehow, I got into an excellent university <u>without</u> doing any homework! I could tell it pissed off my teacher. There were a few other students who seemed incredulous. In fact, it seemed like they were rooting for me to fail.

This provided the motivation I needed. I intended to prove everyone wrong. I wasn't just some "ungifted, dumb ADHD kid." College offered me a clean slate to prove this.

When I began college, there was only one problem...

I Had No Idea How to Study!

I was forced to learn the hard way—through trial and error. Yet, I didn't have time to figure things out. I needed to succeed—and I needed to succeed fast!

In this state I (very quickly) learned the best system for studying. It resulted in straight A's. It wasn't sexy. But it was simple: I showed up to every class, took notes <u>by hand</u>, and then locked myself in the library (without a computer or other distractions). While sitting in the library, I would create 3x5" notecards for what I had just learned. I then quizzed myself on those notecards.[1]

With this process, I ended up graduating *magna cum laude*, with a 3.76 GPA. I also earned a triple emphasis in finance, management, and marketing.

This taught me the power of hard work, focus, and writing by hand.

However, it also taught me one more thing...

**In Order to Succeed,
You Must Love "The Process"**

Even though I had pursued college with the motivation of proving to others that I wasn't "ungifted," in doing so, I learned that I actually loved **the process** of reading, writing, and learning. I loved it so much, in fact, that **I desired a life where I could read, write, and learn—while also getting paid for it.**

---

[1] A process known as "rote learning," or what memory scientists call "maintenance rehearsal."

After a year of working in the "real world," I saw it wasn't the life I wanted. I didn't like working at the tech startup. It entailed pointless meetings, unnecessarily long hours, and dealing with a plethora of "people problems."

I desired a quieter life. One where I could work for myself—as a "solopreneur." I didn't want the Gary Vaynerchuck type of life (you know—where you post 100 pieces of content every day, seven days a week). I didn't want to be glued to my phone. I didn't want to "hustle" on weekends. In brief, I didn't want to be a #HustleCultureBro (pronounced "hashtag-hustle-culture bro").[2] Most important of all...

I Desired to Write!

I felt compelled to write—I wanted to create bodies of written work that made a lasting impact on people. **I wanted to deliver value for the types of people I value.** I had no desire to become "Instagram famous." In fact, I wanted the exact opposite! I wanted to repel everyone other than my core tribe of 1,000 true fans.[3]

---

2 See the Glossary at the back of this book for a full definition.

3 The concept of "1,000 true fans" will be covered in detail later on in this book.

Looking back now, it's clear what I _really_ desired. **I wanted to make six figures a year, writing one thing a month.** I wanted my days to be filled with the same tools I had at my disposal in college: a **pen,** some **notecards, and my brain!** This lifestyle is something the French intellectual monk Antonin Sertillanges called...

"The Intellectual Life"[4]

Here's what the intellectual life looks like...

---

[4] He penned a fantastic book by the same name. See Antonin Sertillanges, *The Intellectual Life: Its Spirit, Conditions, Methods*. (Washington, D.C.: The Catholic University of America Press, 1992).

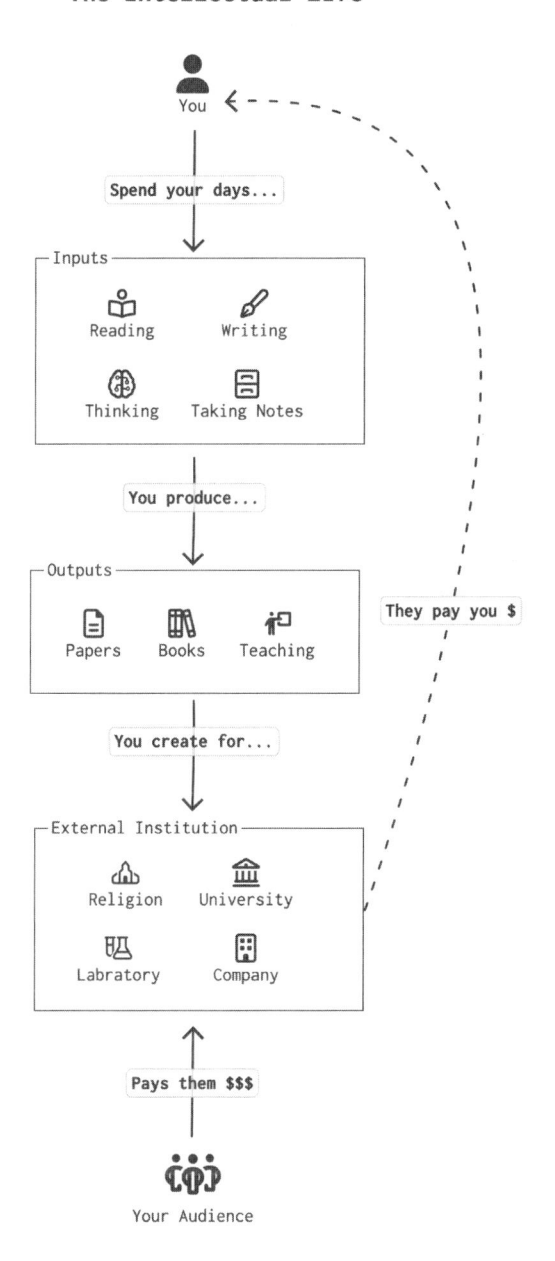

Desires / 47

The Intellectual Life

```
                    You
                     │
              Spend your days...
                     ▼
    ┌─ Inputs ──────────────────┐
    │   Reading      Writing    │
    │   Thinking   Taking Notes │
    └───────────────────────────┘
                     │
              You produce...
                     ▼
    ┌─ Outputs ─────────────────┐
    │  Papers   Books  Teaching │
    └───────────────────────────┘
                     │
              You create for...
                     ▼
    ┌─ External Institution ────┐
    │  Religion    University   │              They pay you $
    │  Labratory   Company      │
    └───────────────────────────┘
                     ▲
                Pays them $$$
                     │
                Your Audience
```

With the intellectual life, you spend your days reading, writing, and thinking. You provide output in the form of research papers, books, and teaching. You provide this for **external institutions** (e.g., universities, religious institutions, research labs, and publishing houses).

I had no interest in pursuing the academic route. Why? Because I saw what that path looked like firsthand. The other options (e.g., publishing houses, research labs, or becoming a Catholic monk) didn't interest me either. They lacked the freedom I desired.

I wanted something *like* the intellectual life—but—instead of providing value to external institutions, I wanted to provide value directly to my audience. Furthermore, I wanted to spend most of my time writing! With the intellectual life, you're **forced** to teach (by giving lectures and sermons). I only wanted to teach if (1) I was passionate about the subject, (2) I knew it would greatly benefit people, and (3) the monetary rewards were very significant.[5]

I wanted something called...

"The Neo-Intellectual Life"

---

5 By "very significant," I mean several millions of dollars per year.

Desires / 49

Here's what the neo-intellectual life looks like:

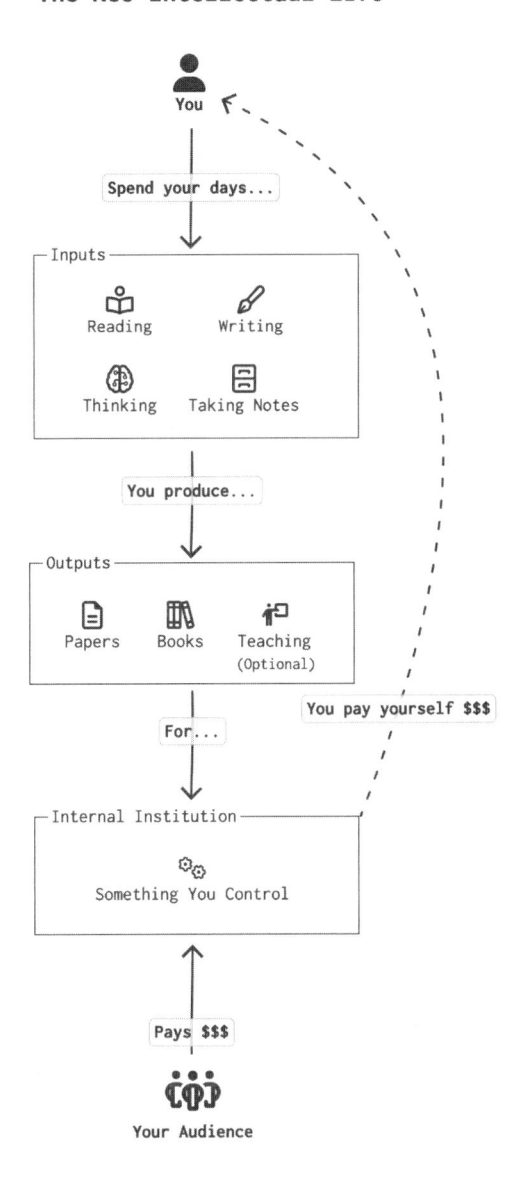

The Neo-Intellectual Life

```
                        You
                         │
                 Spend your days...
                         ↓
      ┌─ Inputs ──────────────────────┐
      │                               │
      │    Reading        Writing     │
      │                               │
      │    Thinking    Taking Notes   │
      └───────────────────────────────┘
                         │
                   You produce...
                         ↓
      ┌─ Outputs ─────────────────────┐
      │                               │
      │   Papers    Books   Teaching  │
      │                    (Optional) │
      └───────────────────────────────┘
                         │
                       For...                You pay yourself $$$
                         ↓
      ┌─ Internal Institution ────────┐
      │                               │
      │      Something You Control    │
      └───────────────────────────────┘
                         ↑
                     Pays $$$
                         │
                   Your Audience
```

With the neo-intellectual life, you spend your days reading, writing, thinking, and taking notes. You produce papers and books and (optionally) teach. However, instead of producing intellectual property for external institutions, you produce it for yourself (your own institution).

As a result of <u>not</u> relying on external institutions, you experience two benefits: **First, you acquire more <u>freedom</u>.** Ask anyone who works for an academic institution. They're in constant fear of losing their job. That, my friend, is <u>not</u> freedom. **Second, you <u>earn</u> <u>more</u>. Why? Because external institutions take a <u>massive</u> cut of what your audience pays.**[6]

When I thought about this, it became clear what I <u>really</u> desired. I desired...

The Neo-Intellectual Life!

At this point, I got clear on what I <u>really</u> wanted. Sure, I wanted to make enough to pay

---

6   Did you know that only 34% of college tuition goes towards benefiting the student by way of instruction? Of that 34% tuition, only a fraction of that goes towards paying the instructor. This is hogwash! When you cut out external institutions, it means more value is attained for <u>both</u> the student and the instructor. See "How Much Do Colleges and Universities Spend on Different Types of Expenses?" IES: National Center for Education Statistics (National Center for Education Statistics).

my mortgage—but even more important was the manner in which I did so. I didn't want a life spent "hustling," I wanted to spend my time reading, writing, and thinking. I wanted to deliver value to the types of people I value.

This stands as a critical step in your journey. If the only thing driving you is *external* (i.e., monetary rewards), you're going to last *maybe* eighteen months—tops. However, if the thing driving you is **internal** (i.e., spending time in your *Zone of Genius* and delivering value to the types of people you value), then you're going to succeed.[7] Why? Because you've built an *antifragile* foundation that will carry you through times when things get tough.[8]

At this point, I had clarity on what my *internal* motivation was. What happened next is a series of mistakes I see many people make—even to this day.

---

7 For more on the concept of "Zone of Genius," see Gay Hendricks, *The Big Leap: Conquer Your Hidden Fear and Take Life to the Next Level*, (New York: HarperOne, 2010).

8 An important exercise to do at some point is called **The Perfect Average Day**. Simply grab a pen and piece of paper and write out what your perfect average day looks like—in detail! From the second you get up, to the second you go to bed. Every detail. Credit for this exercise goes to legendary marketer, Frank Kern.

I want you to read every word of the next chapter. By doing so, you'll save yourself years of wasting time traveling down false paths.

Chapter Four

False Paths

I was familiar with the paths most writers follow to make an independent living. For instance, *freelancing* on websites like *Upwork*. However, freelancing didn't appeal to me. I saw it as a glorified 9-to-5 job <u>without</u> the stability.

I then looked into *blogging*. I set up a *WordPress* blog and added *Google AdSense*. My blog grew quite sizably, but the monetization was laughable—after 100,000 unique visits, I ended up making pennies.

I then switched to the *digital newsletter* model (think platforms like *Medium*, *Ghost*, and *Substack*). In this model, you create free content—and then—you make certain posts available to paying subscribers only. I tried this model and it also didn't work. It turned out people didn't want to pay for text-based content (which is normally free online). Digital articles are free 99.99% of the time. When you're asking people to pay for access to such media, they're one mouse-click away from allocating their attention somewhere else.[1]

I then tried the *copywriting* route. This was similar to the freelancing route—but even worse! One of the greatest copywriters who ever lived, the late, great Gary Halbert, puts it best:

"Honestly, being a copywriter is worse than being a prostitute. A prostitute only gives away their body for an hour. As a copywriter, you not only give away your body, you give away your mind. You give away your heart and soul to your client's market—and you do so for months—if not years! As a copywriter, you literally have to live in the shoes of your client's customers for an ungodly amount of time.

---

[1] I surveyed this landscape recently and here's what I found: The only people making this route work are those with massive audiences—usually politically driven—and even with this, their revenue numbers aren't that great (especially compared to the other business models out there). For instance, "Astral Codex Ten" is one of the top ten digital newsletters out there. It has 5,993 subscribers and an average subscription price of $3.50. That comes out to $20,975.50/month. Not bad, you're thinking. But he's in the top ten out of 15,000+ digital newsletters. In other words, there's a 0.066% chance you can attain the same results. In entrepreneurship, it's normal to have the odds stacked against you (for instance, a 20% chance of success). But such odds come with a reward of millions of dollars a year. With the digital newsletter odds, the probability of success is effectively zero, and the "best case scenario" is $20,000 per month. In brief, this model does not have a healthy risk-reward ratio.

Only then can you truly understand the psyche of the customer."[2]

You see, as a copywriter, your job centers around one thing: **written persuasion**. Your job is to write for clients <u>as if you were them</u>. You're then tasked with entering the conversation going on in the back of <u>their</u> customer's minds.

If your client's customers are horoscope hippies who want to lose weight by eating Ruffles and stroking a rabbit's foot, well then—guess what? You're going to need to spend months living inside the mind of that customer!

The challenge of this is fun (at first). But soon you realize how everything you've created doesn't belong to you. Once you craft an incredible ad campaign, you wake up the next day and have to search for another client.

Here's the reality: 96% of clients who hire copywriters are selling piss-poor products. Seriously! **They're selling stupid products designed to bilk stupid people out of stupid money.** (It's the hard truth.)

---

2   Gary Halbert, "The Root Canal Seminar."

Look—I appreciate the _craft_ of copywriting (and you should, too)—but doing it for others who don't believe in the quality of their own products gets old. Fast.

There are programs out there that glorify copywriting. They say, "You can make a living writing for brands you love!" However, what they _really_ mean is selling your soul on Upwork to clients who want to pay you as little as humanly possible![3] Trust me, you do _not_ want this type of life.

After experiencing the dead-end of copywriting, I enrolled in several online courses. Here's what I learned...

First, the courses that cost practically nothing weren't worth it. You could learn more in an hour by Googling things online.

Second, the higher-end courses were OK—but, in reality, I discovered that many course creators really didn't _do_ the stuff they were teaching. (They made their money by _selling courses about_ the topics they were teaching—instead of doing it themselves.)

---

[3] As Naval Ravikant once said, "You're not going to get rich renting out your time." See Eric Jorgenson, *The Almanack Of Naval Ravikant* (Liberty Publishing, 2022), 31.

I Found This Infuriating!

I didn't want to be a "coach" or "course creator." I simply wanted to *write* for a living.

I learned that coaching, consulting, and running courses were fine as <u>complementary strategies</u>—but I didn't want to be on Zoom for eight hours a day. I wanted *freedom*. I learned that freedom comes by way of **permissionless leverage**.

There are two dominant means of *permissionless leverage*: (1) coding, and (2) writing. The renowned venture capitalist Naval Ravikant says, "If you can't code, then write books."[4] With this in mind, it became clear to me that—my path to freedom would revolve around writing. It was at that point I decided to pursue the neo-intellectual life.

One of my mantras is: *"The only right answer is test."* It reminds me of the importance of experimentation. You may *think* you know, but until you test, you don't *really* know. Thus, the more you experiment, the more you learn.

---

4 For more on "permissionless leverage" and the tapestry of ideas unpacked in this paragraph, see Jorgenson, *The Almanack Of Naval Ravikant*, 34ff.

At this point in my journey, I learned many hard lessons. I followed the paths many independent writers and entrepreneurs take, all of which led me to dead ends.

It's important to test, but it's also important to have short "feedback loops." Some of these false paths took me weeks, while others took me many months. You must remember—I was still working at my day job. I had limited free time. This meant it was more costly to experience the feedback loop of failure.

The important thing is—I knew what I wanted: the neo-intellectual life. This was possible because I got clear on my *internal desires* (which I outlined in Chapter 3). Because of this, I didn't quit when things got hard. I kept going.

At this point I covered the paths of **freelancing**, **blogging**, **digital newsletters**, **copywriting**, **coaching**, **consulting**, and **courses**. Trust me, these are not the paths you want to start out on. They can *complement* your core business model, but they should not be the first thing you build.

Before moving on, you may have noticed that I did not cover one path that is very popular. This is the path we'll explore in the next chapter.

Chapter Five

The Spark

Around this period, something happened that turned everything on its head. On my hour-long commute to the office, I was listening to a podcast about "passive income strategies." The host introduced a new monetization vehicle for independent writers—something called...

Kindle Direct Publishing ("KDP")

Using *Kindle Direct Publishing* (or *"KDP"*), all I had to do was write a book and upload it to Amazon's platform. From there, it would be available in the Kindle bookstore (with millions of customers).

With KDP, it seemed I wouldn't have to worry about things like marketing, setting up a website, payment processing, or any of that stuff! All I had to do was write a book and let Amazon take care of the rest.

I also learned Amazon had just acquired an audiobook platform called *Audible*. This meant I could convert the book into an audio file and add another revenue stream to my book.

This monetization strategy falls into a category called ***digital publishing.***

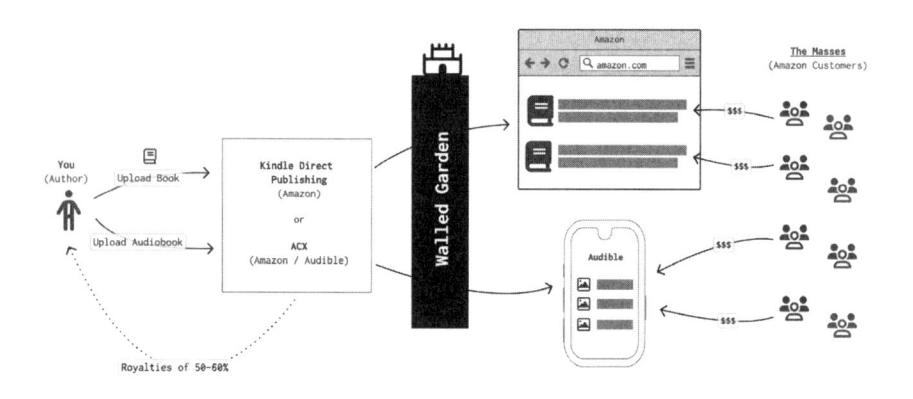

Digital Publishing

There are two defining characteristics of digital publishing:

(1) Walled-Garden Distribution. Even though most people think they're "self-publishing," when they sell their books on Amazon, they're not. They're actually "Amazon-publishing." **Amazon is the one publishing your book, not you.** They're making it available in _their_ _own_ walled garden.

They keep all of your customer data and, in return, they promise exposure to their "masses" of customers.

(2) Digital-Driven Media. The second characteristic is a focus on digital content. Amazon's KDP primarily focuses on digital books and digital audiobooks. There is a print-on-demand option, but it's almost an afterthought.

Here are the defining features of digital publishing:

	Digital Publishing
Audience Size	Mass
Customer PII	No
Transaction Type	One-Time
Marketing	Self-Serve
Payment Processing	External
Royalty Percentage	35-60%

Let's break these down...

- *Audience Size* refers to the size of the market your book is distributed into. With digital publishing, once you publish your book, it will be made available to millions of Amazon readers (i.e., the "masses").

- *Customer PII* refers to "Personally Identifiable Information." With digital publishing, you do not obtain the PII of your readers. Thus, there's no need for things like a customer database to store information.

- *Transaction Type* refers to the nature of purchases. With digital publishing, the reader is purchasing your book once (i.e., a "one-time transaction").

- *Marketing* refers to how you broadcast your book to the masses. With digital publishing, you're responsible for making sure all the marketing copy is written. You do this via a "self-serve" portal on Amazon KDP.

- *Payment Processing* refers to how you process customer orders. With digital publishing, Amazon takes care of payment processing (including refunds). It's "external" to your sphere of responsibilities.

- *Royalty Percentage.* With digital publishing, you offload a lot of administrative tasks. In exchange, the platform takes a large cut of your revenue. On KDP, you get between 35-60% of the sales you generate.

After looking at these tradeoffs, I determined digital publishing was perfect for me. It gave me a new sense of hope. That day,

I arrived at work and felt great. I felt like the neo-intellectual life was around the corner.

After learning about Amazon KDP, I believed—and I mean *seriously* believed—that digital publishing was the missing piece I needed. In order to attain the neo-intellectual life, I would plug Amazon KDP into the model. Here's what it would look like:

The Neo-Intellectual Life
(Digital Publishing)

You

Spend your days...

Inputs
- Reading
- Writing
- Thinking
- Taking Notes

You produce...

Outputs
- Papers
- Books
- Teaching (Optional)

You get paid $$

For...

Internal Institution

Digital Publishing

Amazon KDP

Pays $$$

At this point, I discovered the most viable "monetization vehicle" for myself. At the time of this writing, KDP is _still_ the route most independent writers travel down.

You now have an idea of the KDP model and its defining features. What happened next in my journey is something many of you have experienced. When the rubber meets the road, you learn of details you hadn't foreseen. Soon, a familiar voice begins to creep into your mind...

Chapter Six

Doubts

Soon, I felt a familiar voice enter my mind. On my hour-long commute to the office, I began thinking about the obstacles I'd encounter. It wasn't long before my mind was filled with doubt.

You must understand—at this time, I believed I was my own worst enemy. I had "paralysis by analysis." I was an analytical thinker. I grew overwhelmed thinking about all the steps involved. I began thinking about book formatting, cover design, and—of course—the challenges of writing a book itself!

I also found myself ambivalent about what topic I wanted to write about. I had so many varying interests. **My interests usually only lasted 12-18 months.** Eventually, I grew <u>bored</u> of topics and moved on. The bottom line was...

I Needed to Figure Out My Niche!

I thought to myself, if I focus on one niche as everyone advises, then I'll be known for that niche forever. If I decide to write about a topic like "Google AdWords," then I'll forever be known as "The Google AdWords Guy." I didn't like that. **I wasn't ready to commit to one niche for the rest of my life!**

Furthermore, if I decided to go "all in" on just one niche, **I'd be opening myself up to the embarrassment of things not working out.** My friends from college had landed well-paying jobs at prestigious investment firms. If they visited my LinkedIn and saw I was working on a book, they'd be skeptical—and if I failed, I'd be confirming their beliefs. Frankly, I just wasn't confident I'd succeed. I kept imagining conversations they'd have about the crazy idea I had embarked on. I pictured their jeering smiles if I failed.

On top of this, I felt like I knew a lot about certain topics, but I was certainly no "expert" on any of them. I thought to myself, isn't it absurd of me to even write a book on this topic? Who am I to write a book on this? I had a severe case of *imposter syndrome*.

These were some of the doubts that were now creeping in. Oh—and to top it all off, I was working a full-time job. **I had very little time on my hands.**

Despite these doubts...

I Still Believed Digital Publishing Was The Answer!

While researching the model, I came across several people who claimed to be making a lot of money from Kindle Publishing. Their stories seemed credible, too.[1] As a result, I strongly believed in the digital publishing model.

I believed digital publishing would be simple because Amazon would take care of all the shipping, fulfillment, and customer support. I also believed marketing would be simple because Amazon's marketplace was so large. All I had to do was tap into their massive customer base.

Most of all—I was enthralled by the idea of "passive income." Apparently, all I had to do was write my book once and collect earnings forever. On top of it all, publishing on Kindle sounded fun! I could write all day. **I was willing and ready to make it work—scratch that, I was committed to making it work!**

---

1 I later learned the people who were having success with digital publishing were actually inflating their earnings through paid advertising. For instance, they would show a Kindle royalty check of $6,000 (and leave out the fact that it cost $7,000 in paid advertising to generate such numbers).

My sense of confidence came from <u>knowing</u> the digital publishing model was "the answer." This is part of the reason why that—when confronted with contradictory information—I didn't react too well. You'll find out what I mean in the next chapter. It opens the next part of this journey.

{ Part 2 }
Decisions

Chapter Seven

Ignoring The Mormon

During this period, I came across an individual named Russell Brunson. He was someone who had become popular in the "internet marketing world."

Russell was preaching what sounded like the exact opposite of digital publishing. He emphasized two traits a business model must have:

First, Russell preached the importance of building a website you fully own. I would need to buy a website domain. Then, I'd have to figure out the hosting, payments, fulfillment, email autoresponders, support, shipping, and more.

Second, Russell kept ranting about something called a "funnel." It reminded me of the concept of "sales funnels," which wasn't appealing to me.

Russell made some good points, but it sounded complex. Furthermore, Russell came from the internet marketing world—a world I had dabbled in—however, I found the aesthetic to be "scammy"—think websites with bright red text and sensationalistic copywriting ("Discover 1 WEIRD trick for losing 30 pounds in 7 days, GUARANTEED or DOUBLE Your Money Back!").

I was immediately turned off.

Furthermore, I had a difficult time taking Russell seriously. He wouldn't shut up about being a college wrestler, and he seemed like a "goody-two-shoes." To top it all off...

He Was a Mormon!

How can you trust someone who thinks drinking coffee is a sin?![1]

For all of these reasons, I decided to cast aside Russell Brunson's advice. I proceeded to continue on my merry way—pursuing Amazon's digital publishing model.

In this state, I proceeded to do what every entrepreneur must do, which is...

To Take Action!

---

[1] I say this in jest. I like Mormons. But that doesn't hold me back from poking fun!

Chapter Eight

The Digital Publishing Journey

At that point in my life, my greatest constraint was *time*. I didn't have much of it. For this reason, I decided to wake up one hour earlier than I normally did and... **write!**

By writing first thing in the morning, my mind was fresh. I had the energy needed to do what I deemed most important. As a result, I found the rest of the day to be more fulfilling.

I tried many different writing routines in the beginning. What I found most effective was writing by hand. Doing this helped me think even more deeply. I had clearer thoughts. It also killed the threat of distraction. (Writing on a computer means you're one mouse-click away from your attention being hijacked.)

I called my morning writing routine the **hour of power**.[1] I calculated that I'd finish writing

---

[1] I first heard this phrase from Tony Robbins.

my book in six months by sticking to my hour of power.

I now had my writing routine figured out—the only thing left to figure out was...

My Niche!

I needed to determine <u>what</u> my book should be about.[2] As I surveyed successful non-fiction books, it became clear what the key factor was for success. The key revolved around *simplicity*. My book needed to communicate the main idea in the title of the book, and—the title needed to be simple. It needed to be simple because the book needed to <u>clearly</u> communicate how it would help the reader solve a problem.[3]

I had feared focusing on one simple thing. I feared this because I had a tendency to grow bored of topics. Plus, I didn't want to be known as "The XYZ Guy" forever.

---

2   You may be wondering, **"How do you even start writing a book if you don't know what you're writing about?"** That's a good question. It's good because the answer is counterintuitive. You see, the best way to figure out what book to write does not come by way of <u>thinking</u>. It comes by way of <u>doing</u>—and for writers, that comes by way of...<u>writing</u>!

3   This taps into a related phenomenon in cognitive psychology known as the "availability heuristic." A simple book title communicates a simple idea. The simple idea possesses a higher probability of spreading, thus tapping into the phenomenon known as the "availability cascade."

After some time, I decided to cast aside these doubts. It was delaying my progress. I decided to write a book focused entirely on one thing.

Paradoxically, the thing I decided to focus my book on was: *focus*. That's right. I decided to teach strategies for becoming a more "focused" person. I decided to title the book, How to Get Focused.

I now had my niche and title. Next, I began writing the book. After three months, I felt good about my progress. The quality of my writing felt good, too. Things were going so well that I decided to announce my new project publicly. I did this by posting on LinkedIn. I told people I was writing a book about "focus." After posting, I could sense skepticism from my peers, yet I pressed forward anyway.

At the end of six months, I completed the first draft of my book. I then spent another few weeks revising it. I was still dead broke, and I didn't have the budget to pay for a typesetter. However, I negotiated a deal with a designer who agreed to do it for free—as long as I credited him inside the book.

The last step involved getting a cover designed. After a few dead ends, I was able to find a way to get an amazing cover created at an affordable price.[4]

After all of this, I was finally ready. My book was finally complete. It took me seven months in total. I remember thinking to myself, now all I have to do is simply upload my book to Amazon KDP. Soon, the sales will start pouring in!

Before I knew it, I was ready to launch my book. I wish I could say this was a good thing, but... you're about to find out what it _really_ was...

---

4   I used the service called "99 Designs" (which was fairly new at the time).

Chapter Nine

The Launch

I was in a great mood leading up to launch day. My commute to work didn't bother me as much. I figured I would be resigning soon. I expected to make thousands of dollars in royalties from my launch. I pictured walking into my boss's office and telling him I'm resigning. "Why?" he'd ask. To which I'd reply, "To become an independent writer."

I truly believed the neo-intellectual life was around the corner.

Then... launch day came.

My royalty earnings came out to roughly one hundred dollars. In fact, my earnings for the entire month came out to only $135.27!

Here's a screenshot:

These Results Were Awful!

September 2010

Approximated Royalties: $135.27

How to Get Focused: $135.27

Unfortunately, it didn't get any better. Amazon's supposed "masses" of customers never came.[1] The myth of passive income from Amazon was just that—a myth.

Soon, things went from bad to worse.

You see—because my mind had been so preoccupied with my book, my performance at my day job declined. As a result, I ended up getting fired only two weeks after my book launched. Finances were already tight. I had recently purchased a townhouse. Now, I found myself with no job and very little in savings.

---

1   I later learned how generating book sales on KDP relies on Amazon's advertising platform. After trying this route, and optimizing ad campaigns, the results were awful. 96% of the time, you won't turn a profit advertising your book on Amazon; you'll (hopefully) get close to break-even. The only reason people advertise on Amazon is (again hopefully) to attract good reviews. After they get that initial momentum, they can then turn off ads. This is not a healthy strategy.

It wasn't <u>all</u> that bad. The small number of people who purchased my book loved it. This news lifted my spirits. Two people emailed me and emphasized how the book was changing their lives. They also appreciated how well it was written. I thought to myself, at least my writing method seemed to have worked. Also, it seemed like focusing my book on <u>one</u> <u>topic</u> was the right choice.

The problem wasn't my book, nor was it the manner in which I produced it. The problem was...

Amazon's Digital Publishing Model Was Broken!

It was broken for small, independent writers like myself. I had made five dollars in profit per sale. That's nothing. Seriously! That type of payout will <u>never</u> result in wealth (unless you're J.K. Rowling, selling millions of books a year).

I had bet on the wrong business model, and unfortunately, I had no time to "course correct." I had to get a job—**fast**.

At that point, I found myself exhausted. I was tired of writing about focus. I decided to drop my book project and move on.

I had to scramble to pay the bills. Luckily, I landed a job doing marketing for another tech startup.[2] Slowly, I began rebuilding my career.

I carried a lot of "cognitive baggage" from that year. By betting on the digital publishing model, I had burnt myself out. Furthermore, it added a lot of stress to my marriage. Later on, we ended up getting divorced.

I'm sharing this with you to illustrate the **seriousness** of betting on the right business model. If you want to build the neo-intellectual life, there are an endless number of paths you can choose. Most of them lead to a dead end—including Amazon KDP.

Pursuing the wrong business model can have <u>very serious</u> consequences. I experienced a lot of pain and suffering by choosing the wrong path. Due to this experience, I determined that the neo-intellectual life was impossible for all but a few people. This is why, at that point...

I Decided to Abandon The Dream of Making Money From Writing

---

[2] Fun fact: This company was Kajabi, which was only three people at the time. I was their first key hire and helped them grow in the very early days.

Over the following years, I honed my marketing craft. I was generating *a* _lot_ of success for the people I worked with. I founded a company and took it from $0 to $3 million dollars in revenue in less than two years. I thought I knew a lot about marketing. Then, something happened which... turned my world upside down.

Chapter Ten

The Return of the Mormon!

I was attending a marketing conference in San Diego called *Traffic & Conversion Summit*. I grew bored listening to speakers, so I began wandering around the halls. I came upon a booth for a company called *ClickFunnels*. I had heard of ClickFunnels because it was the company Russell Brunson had co-founded. (Russell is the marketer I mentioned earlier whose advice I had previously ignored.) I learned that Russell's company was now generating $100 million in revenue. Furthermore, he had released a new book sharing his strategies.

Clearly, Russell was onto something. Given that I had ignored his advice last time and failed, I figured it might be wise to pay attention to what he was saying this time. Therefore, the next day I decided to purchase his new book.

I started reading his book, and I couldn't put it down. Everything he was saying began to make sense. He taught his concepts via easy-to-follow diagrams, and he backed them up with data.

Previously, Russell had emphasized the importance of "building a website you <u>fully own</u>." I now learned why this was so important, and actually—the reason for why was simple:

Building a Website You Own Enables You to <u>Know</u> Your Customers!

With your own website, you will know your customer's name, email address, phone number, mailing address, and more. This unlocks the potential to have a long-term relationship with every one of your customers.

With Amazon, you have no idea who your customers are, and you only generate one-time transactions from them. After they buy your book, they're gone—likely forever.

You see, by having a <u>direct relationship</u> with your customers, you can launch future products to a raving list of fans, and—you can transact with them over and over and over again.

Russell emphasized that by owning your own website, you can leverage a powerful sequence known as a *funnel*.

Previously, I had found the concept of a "funnel" cringeworthy (reminding me of a "sales funnel"). It also sounded complicated. However, as I read Russell's book, he broke it down in detail and made it simple to understand.

Here's How a Funnel Works...

After a customer purchases your product, you immediately send them to a new page (an *upsell page*). On the upsell page, you offer the customer a *one-time-only offer* (aka, an *"OTO"*). The customer can get the OTO by simply clicking a button that says, "Yes, Add This Product to My Order."

After the customer is finished, they land on a *thank you page* (which contains the order receipt).

Now, let me share a few more important points: First, the OTO is typically priced <u>higher</u> than the product they initially purchased. This means—most of your profit actually comes from your OTO.

Normally, a new customer wouldn't purchase your higher-priced product on their own. Why? Because the higher price typically requires a longer "sales cycle." However, because the person *just purchased* a product from you, they're now in a state of "buyer's heat."[1] As a result, the customer has a significant chance of saying yes to your higher-priced product.[2] This is why funnels are so powerful.

You don't end up turning a profit on the first product your customer purchases (known as a *frontend product*). You actually make your money with your OTO (known as a *backend product*). The frontend product acts as a *tripwire*—that is, it serves as a trigger mechanism that induces buyer's heat in a customer.[3] It serves as the first step that brings people into your world.[4]

---

1   This taps into a cognitive behavior known as the **commitment heuristic**. For more, see Robert B. Cialdini, *Influence: The Psychology of Persuasion*, Rev. ed., (New York, NY: Collins, 2006), see Chapter 3: Commitment and Consistency: Hobgoblins of the Mind.

2   In my experiments, across five different books from different subcategories, I've found that, on average, 25% of people end up saying yes to the OTO on the upsell page.

3   The term "tripwire" is also known as "loss leader," or as Alen Sultanic argues for, a "value vehicle." See Alen Sultanic and Robert Neckelius, *Automatic Clients*, 2021, 40.

4   As an independent writer, researcher, or entrepreneur, one of your core tasks centers on creating your own "world" for people—that is, your own land, language, terms, and more. This is known as "sociological marketing." This runs counter to what most marketers focus on—that being "psychological marketing." For more on this concept, see Ben Settle, *BizWorld: How to Create an Irresistible Business Universe Your Customers Love to Buy from and Hate to Leave* (Independently Published, 2023).

All of this is what Russell meant by a "funnel."

Funnel

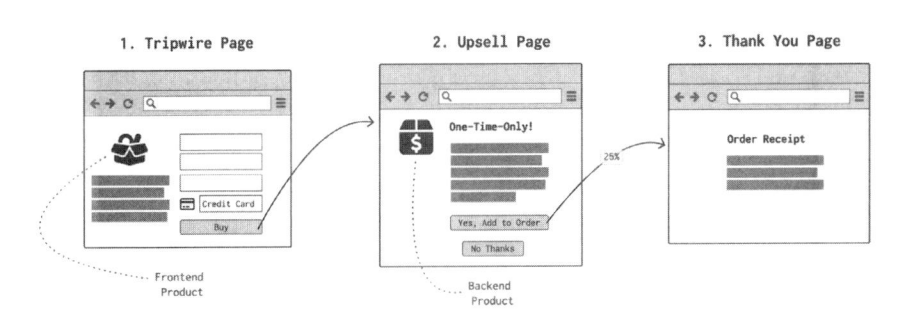

1. Tripwire Page — Frontend Product
2. Upsell Page — One-Time-Only! — Backend Product
3. Thank You Page — Order Receipt

After I learned about funnels, it no longer seemed like a "cringeworthy" internet marketing tactic. Furthermore, the economics of the model made sense. It no longer seemed complicated. Actually, it was quite simple.

After I finished Russell's book, I understood his true power was his strategy (i.e., the strategy of using funnels). When I was first introduced to him, I was turned off by his use of bright-red text on websites. I also didn't care for his sensationalistic headlines. Those were just "tactics." They were probably implemented by some junior copywriter. His strategy, however, was fantastic, and the truth is...

Strategy Supersedes Tactics!

In sum, I learned that I could implement funnels—but, I could do so in a *tasteful* way. This was an important step in my journey. I had learned that the digital publishing model was <u>not</u> the path to freedom.

I learned the intricacies of funnels, and—for the first time—it all made sense. Still, I knew that I would need to be "all in" to have success. Therefore, I had an important decision to make. That's what I'll tell you about next.

Chapter Eleven

A New Hope

Even though Russell's platitudes *still* didn't resonate with me, I found his marketing insights to be profound. I grew to love his enthusiasm and work ethic. In fact, I soon became a fan.

**The Mormon Had Returned,
and God Almighty...
I Accepted Him!**

At this point, I had experienced failure by following Amazon's digital publishing model. I was open and committed to learning. After reading Russell's book, I finally understood why owning your own website was important. It was necessary for building a funnel.

I had experienced pain and suffering by choosing the wrong business model before. But not this time. This time, I decided to follow Russell. I decided to follow his advice, and...

I Decided to Learn
The Ways of "The Funnel"

This is an important step. I allocated a chapter to this for a reason. Before making any significant change, there's a "precursor step." That precursor step is that...

You Must **Decide** to Change!

I remember exactly where I was when I **decided** to learn the ways of the funnel. I had just moved to Encinitas, California. I was living in a house painted green, and I owned two lime-green cars that sat out front.[1] I was in one of the guest rooms reading Russell's book. I mapped out every important concept on notecards. Suddenly, everything clicked for me. I knew that funnels were the path to freedom.

Before making any significant change, you must decide that you are going "all in." Otherwise, you're setting yourself up to fail. Why? Because the path to success is hard. You'll need to push past initial failure and press forward. Entrepreneurship is hard as is.

---

[1] I have an obsession with the color lime green. I have owned many lime-green cars: a Lamborghini Huracán Performante, two lime-green Dodge Challenger Hellcats, a "pimped out" lime-green Jeep Wrangler, and currently, a lime-green Tesla Model S Plaid (the fastest production car ever created).

If you're not <u>committed</u> to success, you'll give up before you experience the fruits of your hard work.

This is precisely what you're about to learn in Part 3 of this book.

Press on!

{ Part 3 }
Trials

Chapter Twelve

The Hidden Power of Analog

Armed with my knowledge of funnels, I decided to put it to the test. I had recently joined a company as its Chief Marketing Officer (a "CMO"). It was a turnaround job. The company had a negative net worth of $2.14 million dollars.[1] They were on the brink of bankruptcy. Why did I decide to join? Because first, the Founder & CEO was a friend, and second, I love challenges. Therefore, I decided to join the company. My goal was to engineer the turnaround of the century.

Here's the first thing I did: I decided to completely reposition the company. They were struggling to stay afloat in the "lost items" space. They created Bluetooth devices that helped find lost items, like keys, in case they

---

1 Known as a "net working deficiency." See "2017 Annual Report—SEC Filings," https://www.sec.gov/Archives/edgar/data/1577351/000119312518143726/d579201dpartii.htm.

go missing. The company's devices were similar to Apple Airtags (but way less reliable and with lots of glitches). It took some time but I eventually got the support needed to shift the company's direction. We shifted into a fast-growing industry and decided to launch a mobile app. I believed this would be the perfect opportunity to test out my new hope (funnels).

I decided to launch a funnel. The *frontend product* would be a free trial of the app, and after they purchased, we would send the customer to an upsell page with a backend product. The backend product would be a one-time-only offer providing them with additional benefits (better in-app rewards and more).

I was confident in this model and a huge believer in the power of funnels. Soon, everything was built. We launched the funnel, and...

It Failed Miserably!

When I analyzed the data, it didn't make any sense. **Why wasn't the funnel converting?** I contacted the people who didn't buy. I asked them why they didn't purchase. They told me they didn't want to enter their credit card info for "yet another app." They told me our offer wasn't unique. "Everyone out there," they said, "is already advertising things like free digital eBooks, digital courses, and free trials of some app." When I observed what the broader marketplace was doing, I realized my customers were right. It occurred to me what the common denominator was...

Everybody Was Advertising <u>Digital</u> Products!

Companies in the marketplace were trying to avoid the hassles that came with selling physical products. They were trying to take the easy way out. They were trying to avoid complications of shipping and fulfillment by only selling things like courses, software, apps, and more. The problem was...

Customers Were Already Inundated With <u>Digital</u> Offers!

Customers didn't want yet another eBook. What they *really* wanted was something **<u>real</u>**— a physical product. I learned that...

Customers Were Starving for <u>ANALOG</u>![2]

---

2 Defined, **"Analog"** refers to physical objects that do not rely on digital software or binary code.

As I mentioned, the company I had joined was originally in the "lost items" space. Therefore, what I did was this: I created a new funnel that gave away one of their Bluetooth devices for free—customers only had to pay for shipping and handling. It also came with a free trial of the app. This was my new frontend product. Then, on the upsell page, everything was the same as before. They received a one-time-only offer, which provided them with additional benefits and in-app rewards.

Guess what happened after I launched this new funnel?

It Was a Massive Success!

In fact, it helped generate $21.6 million dollars in revenue that year. Here's a screenshot:

STATEMENTS OF OPERATIONS

	Year Ended December 31,	
Sales	$ 21,620,577	$ 1,030,389
Cost of sales	(5,640,114)	(800,889)
Gross profit	15,980,463	229,500
Operating expenses:		
Research and development	1,373,122	399,756
Selling and marketing	13,700,104	2,138,235
General and administrative	6,660,627	1,466,531
Intangible asset impairment losses	4,264,899	—
Total operating expenses	25,998,752	4,004,522
Operating loss	(10,018,289)	(3,775,022)
Realized gain	7,953,833	—
Interest expense	(497,761)	(442,534)
Other income	29,790	18,022

That simple funnel ended up turning the company around and saving it from bankruptcy.

The change was simple...

The Funnel Went From Failure to Success By Converting The Frontend Product From <u>Digital</u> to <u>Analog</u>

This was a key breakthrough in my journey. I learned that building a funnel was <u>not</u> enough. I learned the key to success doesn't come from building <u>any</u> type of funnel. **Rather, it's critical you offer an <u>analog</u> product on the frontend of the funnel.** Why? Because everyone is inundated with digital products. Offering customers <u>analog</u> products differentiates you from the crowd.

It's not just about creating a funnel, it's about creating one with an *analog product*. However... I learned pretty quickly that an analog product wasn't enough. There's something else that is necessary for **long-term** success. That's what we'll cover next.

Chapter Thirteen

The Hidden Power of Knowledge

Before agreeing to join the company that operated in the lost items space, I negotiated an equity stake in the business. This allowed me to exit the company (and also exit the chaos that comes with running a 100-person team). Because of the financial success we had, I found myself in a position to make some angel investments. One such investment was in a company in the financial education space. The company was comprised of three founders. I saw a lot of talent in them. However, after nine months, they were struggling to stay afloat. Even though they ran one of the most popular podcasts in their niche, they were failing to generate any revenue. Their situation was dire. <u>Very</u> dire. I remember something that happened to one of the founders—a young lad named Bryce. He was only a few years out of college (and thus had very little in savings). One day, while they were working in their small one-bedroom apartment, Bryce walked in, slammed the door behind him, and sat on the floor. He was dejected. He was stressed and very upset. "What happened?" one of the founders asked Bryce. He responded, "I got a parking ticket. I literally cannot afford to pay it."

They decided to take my advice and build out a funnel. However, when I looked at their newly-built funnel, I saw what the problem was. Their frontend product was for a membership community costing $49.95/month. In other words, they were selling a digital frontend product. They needed a funnel that started with an analog frontend product.

Unlike my previous company, they didn't have a physical product already built. Nor did they have a team to support shipping and fulfillment. This presented a challenge we needed to overcome.

During that period, I was spending much of my time smoking cigars on my balcony while reading. One day, while overlooking the beautiful bay of San Diego, I came upon something interesting. I was reading a book in the field of psychology. It identified the fact that the very first human need is *knowledge*. From the very moment we're born, we find ourselves in a state of disorientation. Our first need is to **know** what is going on.[1]

---

1 Jonathan Cook, *The Perennial Psychology: A Timeless Approach to*

After thinking about this, it suddenly dawned on me what the solution was. The frontend product should <u>not</u> <u>only</u> be analog, it should also help customers <u>orient</u> themselves—that is, it should provide them with **knowledge**. In other words, it should be an **analog <u>knowledge</u> product.** What is an analog knowledge product? Analog knowledge products are things like books, guides, templates, cheat sheets, and more—with the key distinction that... they're delivered in analog form.

Around this time, I learned that the sales of the previous company I exited had started to decline. This made me begin to recognize the importance of providing <u>knowledge</u> to customers. You see, my previous company had offered a Bluetooth device as their analog product. This did nothing to create <u>loyalty</u> in their customers. People ended up being enticed by the free Bluetooth device and stayed customers for a short period of time. However, they eventually switched to other apps. Their analog funnel worked, but only in the short term.

My hypothesis was that by creating an analog knowledge product, we could **indoctrinate** customers. That is, we would provide incredible value <u>and</u> get them emotionally involved in our mission. In doing so, we would build long-term

---

Understanding Human Nature (LiveReal LLC, 2020), 145ff.

customer loyalty, and this would pay off in the long run. Again, "indoctrinating" customers is something that is made possible by an *analog knowledge product*, not merely an *analog product*.

With this in mind, we embarked on the project of creating an ***analog book*** shipped to the doorsteps of customers. I was an "active" angel investor at the time. Therefore, I decided to spearhead the project. The three founders of the company were not the best writers out there. Therefore, I hired one of the best ghostwriters I knew. We all spent the day in a conference room with whiteboards. We outlined the table of contents. Then, the three founders spoke and taught their ideas. Meanwhile, the ghostwriter recorded everything. One month later, the book was finished.[2] Shortly thereafter, we launched the funnel and...

It Was an Immediate Success!

---

[2] Note: My personal workflow for writing books revolves around analog. That is, I write my books by hand. Many other authors follow this practice as well because it results in better writing. However, I understand that this is not viable for certain types of people (e.g., busy entrepreneurs). That's fine. There are actually several ways to create excellent books without writing a single word yourself. The most important thing is "Value Per Page" (VPP). Don't fill your book with gibberish, and—please, for the love of God—do not fill it with ChatGPT garbage.

That funnel has ended up doing over $25 million dollars in revenue. It completely changed the founders' lives. Seriously! Bryce later joked, "I remember those days—the good old days—when I was one parking ticket away from being wiped out financially."

The company is still thriving five years later.[3] They're even more profitable than the previous company I had exited.

My hypothesis was correct. Analog knowledge products <u>indoctrinate</u> customers. The book they created resulted in a loyal base of fans that have stuck by their side. They have experienced long-term success, thanks to their analog knowledge product.

The lesson is simple...

Analog <u>Knowledge</u> Products Are Better Than Plain Analog Products

This was a subtle yet important discovery in my journey. *Analog knowledge products* trump plain old *analog products*. Why? Because they <u>indoctrinate</u> customers and create life-long fans.

---

3 Their success makes me very happy, not only because I like the founders, but also because I get a <u>very</u> nice dividend check every year!

Yet, analog knowledge products aren't enough. They're critical for <u>getting</u> customers. But there's something else you need in order to <u>monetize</u> customers. That's what we'll cover next.

Chapter Fourteen

The Final Hidden Power

At that point in my life, I had generated $73 million dollars in revenue, and $44 million dollars in profit for my businesses. Here's a screenshot:

Row Labels	Sum of Gross Profit	Sum of Revenue
Year-1	$1,035,607.00	$2,759,322.00
Year-2	$1,710,086.38	$7,563,066.65
Year-3	$2,100,228.52	$5,501,676.00
Year-4	$602,402.82	$1,621,650.69
Year-5	$960,607.95	$1,782,723.13
Year-6	$309,094.58	$850,601.31
Year-7	$25,373,401.35	$36,824,985.18
Year-8	$12,435,951.00	$16,270,632.00
Grand Total	$44,527,379.60	$73,174,656.96

I realized then that—this amounts to more money than what most of the "gurus" whose advice I was listening to had made. I had basically hit the financial goals they motivated me to strive for—and in fact—I had far surpassed many of them!

While all of this may sound impressive to you, it was *the worst* thing that ever happened to me. In fact...

It Literally Wrecked My Life

When I hit those financial goals, I thought I'd feel like I was in heaven. But in reality— I found myself straight in the depths of hell. The fact is...

I Was a Burnt-Out Workaholic!

The business models I had been chasing had destroyed most of the important relationships that mattered to me. I had no personal life, and I was always "hustling." I had to *constantly* communicate with my audience, *constantly* check social media, and *constantly* create new products.

This prompted me to go into "early retirement." I decided to take time off from working. I had been grinding nonstop for twelve years. The stress of turning around the Bluetooth company left me exhausted. I no longer wanted to "grind." I no longer wanted to be a CMO tasked with epic turnarounds. I wanted to do something *fulfilling*! I wanted to read, write, and think all day—and, I wanted to make a fantastic living doing so. I once again began finding myself called to...

The Neo-Intellectual Life

During my "early retirement," like I said, I spent most of my days smoking cigars. I also spent a lot of time reading. My favorite things to read were newsletters from Gary Halbert, the best copywriter who ever lived. I purchased two thick binders containing all of the newsletters he wrote in the '80s and '90s. (It cost me close to $1,000.) Each newsletter was only 8-12 pages, and yet they contained some of the most valuable pieces of wisdom I had ever read. Truthfully, these newsletters helped me get through a very dark period of my life.

There was something special about reading these old-school newsletters. A key part of the experience was that they were in *analog* form. There's a special connection you get when reading something in analog form. It's something that does not emerge by staring at your phone.[1]

---

1   Author David Sax puts it nicely: "Even though the content of an article in

There's the special "smell" of the pages and a special feel when turning pages. It triggers something memory scientists call *external context*.[2] In essence, the physical elements involved in learning—including location, environment, sounds, smells, tastes, and texture—end up increasing the *depth* of the material's "imprint" on your mind.[3] This is a very important point. **Your writing will have a far deeper impact on readers by offering it to them in analog form.**

Thanks in part to the analog nature of Gary Halbert's newsletters, he ended up creating one of the largest collections of "superfans" in the marketing world at the time. Seriously—his newsletter made him one of the most famous

---

the print edition of *The Economist* is the exact same as one I can read on the publications website or app, the digital experience lacks the smell of the ink, the sound of the page crinkling, the texture of the paper on my fingers. These may seem irrelevant to the way an article is consumed, but they aren't." Cf. David Sax, The Revenge of Analog, 111.

2   Michael Jacob Kahana, *Foundations of Human Memory* (New York: Oxford University Press, 2014), 12ff.

3   McGeoch, JA. "Forgetting and the law of disuse." Psychological Review, 39, 365. "The learner is forming associations, not only intrinsic to the material which is being learned, but also between the parts of this material and the manifold features of the context or environment in which the learning is taking place."

marketers alive. Gary's analog newsletter positively impacted legions of people and it continues to do so—even today! This got me thinking...

Could I Resurrect The Lost Art of Analog Newsletters?

By doing this, I could create a tribe of 1,000 true fans. This is the key to making a fantastic living as an independent writer. I thought to myself, perhaps I could finally create the neo-intellectual life. However, due to my previous failure with Kindle publishing, I wasn't confident that making money as an independent writer was even possible. Then, I heard something that changed everything...

I was living in downtown San Diego at the time. In order to escape the concrete city, I made it a daily habit to get out into nature. My spot of choice was a natural park located inland from *SeaWorld* called "Tecolote Canyon." On a Monday afternoon in November, I was on my daily run through Tecolote Canyon. I was listening to a podcast by Russell Brunson. He was talking about what he'd do if he were to start over from scratch. He revealed he'd implement the business model of someone named "Ben Settle." Ben's business model was simple: he wrote an ***analog monthly newsletter***. That was Ben's entire business. Seriously! Ben had been doing this consistently for over a decade. After doing some research, I learned...

Ben Was Averaging Over $700,000 a Year Thanks to His Analog Monthly Newsletter![4]

After analyzing Ben's business model, it became clear why it worked so well. It worked so well because it's built on **recurring revenue**. That is, you acquire a customer once and they join your monthly subscription. Each month, your subscriber base grows and you end up experiencing the magical effects of **compounding** (i.e., what Charlie Munger refers to as "The Eighth Wonder of The World").

This Is The Hidden Power of Analog Monthly Newsletters

The main lesson here is that you want an *analog knowledge product* with *recurring revenue*. In other words, you want an **analog monthly newsletter**.

At this point in my journey, everything really started coming together. I first learned

---

4   According to Ben, he generated $9.3 million from 2009 to 2022. This comes out to an average of $715,384.62 per year. For more, see: Ben Settle, "Confessions of a Lowly $9.3 Million Copywriter."

the power of *funnels*. Then, the power of *analog products*. Soon afterward, I learned the power of *analog knowledge products*. The last piece was *analog monthly newsletters*. This was the key. Without this final piece, the neo-intellectual life would be impossible. Without the analog monthly newsletter, one is forced to subsidize their freedom by taking on responsibility from some external provider (such as an academic institution).

The analog publishing revolution was just getting started...

Chapter Fifteen

Analog Publishing Revolution

Over the following months, I began to spot a pattern I had previously overlooked. There was a small group of underground writers who were making a killer living with analog knowledge products.[5]

This group had an approach that ran counter to the digital publishing model. Instead of focusing on *masses* of nameless customers (like Kindle publishing), this group focused on serving a *tiny* group of customers whom they knew and liked. In other words, they focused on serving their...

"1,000 True Fans."

---

5 For instance, the following publications: "Cereal," "Little Brother," "Kinfolk," "Lucky Peach," "Drift" (coffee and travel), "California Sunday," "Girls, Guns and Rods," and more. For more, see: David Sax, *The Revenge of Analog: Real Things and Why They Matter*, (New York: PublicAffairs, 2016), 104ff.

The theory of *1,000 true fans* originated from the founding editor of *Wired* magazine.[6] In essence, you only need 1,000 "true fans" to make a living from your intellectual work. These 1,000 true fans serve as the lifeblood of the work you publish—they purchase anything and everything you release and are with you to the bitter end. **In brief, the only thing you need to focus on is cultivating a tribe of 1,000 true fans!**

I noticed that those who created analog knowledge products did this differently. Instead of following the hype, this group went in the complete opposite direction. Instead of creating digital products and eBooks, they stuck with the analog medium. Instead of digital publishing, they operated within the category of...

"Analog Publishing"

Here is a comparison of the two models:

---

6   Kevin Kelly, "1,000 True Fans," The Technium.

	Digital Publishing	Analog Publishing
Audience Size	Mass	Tiny
Customer PII	No	Yes
Transaction Type	One-Time	Recurring
Marketing	Self-Serve	Self-Serve
Payment Processing	External	Internal
Royalty Percentage	35-60%	100%

Let's break this down...

- *Audience Size.* With analog publishing, the focus is serving a *tiny* audience of *1,000 true fans*. The point is to focus on your true passions (not whatever the market desires). In doing so, you'll attract your tiny dream audience and repel the rest.

- *Customer PII.* With analog publishing, you build relationships with your customers. You grow to *know* them, *like* them, and *trust* them. As such, you build a valuable customer database that contains your customers' information (name, address, birthdays, and more).

- *Transaction Type.* With analog publishing, a customer doesn't just purchase once. They make recurring purchases—ideally, recurring <u>monthly</u> purchases. You end up acquiring a customer once and transacting with them <u>forever</u>.

- **Marketing.** The myth of Amazon taking care of the marketing for you is just that—a myth. With analog publishing, just like digital publishing, you yourself are responsible for marketing. However, because you own your own website, you'll have even more control.

- **Payment Processing.** With analog publishing, you'll need to set up your own payment processor. This is dead simple these days. In fact, it's a one-click toggle for most website platforms.

- **Royalty Percentage.** With analog publishing, you retain 100% of the royalties your book generates (minus a small processing fee).[7]

After my failed experience with digital publishing, I understood the *real* tradeoffs between the two business models. At first glance, it may seem like analog publishing requires more work, but that's a fallacy. (I'll show you why in a moment.) The most important

---

[7] At the time of this writing, Stripe charges 2.9%. This cut is a whole lot better than what Amazon takes (40-65%). Heck, even Amazon's cut isn't *that* bad compared to traditional publishers, which can ~~steal~~ take over 90%!

thing you should be looking at is the <u>effectiveness</u> of the business model.

After understanding the nature of digital publishing vs. analog publishing, it was clear which one was the winner: *analog publishing*.

At this point, I started to see patterns emerge. I discovered an **entirely new category** of monetization. I knew the neo-intellectual life would be achieved through this new category—analog publishing.

However, I noticed varying degrees of success between analog publishers. Some were experiencing <u>significant</u> wealth, while others were struggling to survive.

What was the key to unlocking financial success within analog publishing? That is what we'll explore next.

Chapter Sixteen

The One Funnel to Rule Them All

As I surveyed the landscape of analog publishers, I saw a positive sign: many of them were profitable. This was <u>not</u> the case for digital publishers. However, the levels of success between each analog publisher varied. **I identified <u>three requirements</u> necessary for having massive success within analog publishing.** Some had one or two of these, but very few had <u>all three</u>.

Without further ado, here are the three requirements:

<u>Requirement #1</u>: A Funnel

As you know, a funnel involves two things: (1) a tripwire page promoting a frontend product, and (2) an upsell page promoting a one-time-only offer (an "OTO").

I had known about funnels for a long time,

but I had never taken them seriously until I finally listened to Russell Brunson. After putting funnels to the test, I learned how critical they were. Funnels induce **buyer's heat**. This enables you to sell more products immediately, which skyrockets the **Average Order Value** ("AOV") of transactions.

When I analyzed the business models of other analog publishers, I noticed most of them did not have a funnel! Many simply used *Shopify* websites to sell analog books. As a result, they were slightly profitable, but still struggling. Their margins were nowhere near where they could (or should) be.

This brings us to the second requirement:

Requirement #2: Analog Knowledge Tripwire

An analog knowledge tripwire includes things like physical books, guides, or reports that you sell as a frontend product.

My experience helping the financial education company taught me that tripwires should not only be *analog products*, they should be *analog knowledge products* (for instance, an analog book). Analog books **indoctrinate** readers. They turn customers into life-long fans.[1]

---

[1] The Founder of Behance (a digital platform for designers) began producing

Furthermore, there is *intrinsic value* baked into analog books. People <u>love</u> buying books. It doesn't take much effort to sell books. This is why they work so well as a tripwire.

Yet, when I surveyed the landscape of analog publishers, I noticed something peculiar. **Most people tried to cut corners.** For instance, one individual who operated an analog monthly newsletter was selling a book—but it was an eBook. When I investigated why he was doing this, his reasoning was: "During COVID, it made shipping and fulfilling physical books difficult. Therefore, I switched over to selling an eBook and I didn't notice much of a drop in the conversion rate."

Sure, this was a valid excuse during COVID, but at the time I'm writing this, it's been many years since COVID—and he's *still* using an eBook!

Oh well, perhaps he's still using an eBook because, as he said, it didn't hurt his conversion rate. I could have taken his word at face value (but of course, I didn't!). I decided to investigate his tripwire page, and I saw why his

---

analog knowledge products. According to him, "People who have purchased any of those physical products have gone on to become the most fervent ambassadors for the Behance community in ways that digital products (eBooks, online seminars, virtual notebooks) would never foster." Cf. David Sax, *The Revenge of Analog*, 218.

conversion rate hadn't dropped. On his tripwire page, he made it **extremely unclear** as to what type of book it was. It was unclear whether you were getting a physical book or an eBook. On his page, he uses an image of a physical book. In reality, there is *not* *one* mention of the word "eBook." It only mentions a "digital book," and it's buried at the bottom of the page.

After I finished purchasing his book, I got an email with a link to a PDF. This was underwhelming. I was misled into thinking I was getting a physical book by paying $4.99. Instead, I got a lousy PDF!

This is *not* the way you want to start out a new customer relationship. He lost my *trust*. This tactic defeats the whole purpose of selling a book in the first place! You see...

The Purpose of Selling a Book Is NOT to Make Money!

That's right. The purpose of a book is to build **KLT** with customers. That is, you want them to *Know*, *Like*, and *Trust* you. That way, they'll become rabid buyers of future products you offer them.

The lesson here? Don't cut corners. **If you want to have success, do things right—use an** _**analog knowledge product**_. If you're concerned about the difficulty of printing, shipping, and fulfillment, don't worry. I'll show you a way to sell analog books that makes things as simple as selling an eBook—where all the logistics are taken care of for you.

This brings us to the third requirement:

Requirement #3: Analog Monthly Newsletter

An _analog monthly newsletter_ is a piece of knowledge you mail to people's doorsteps every month.

I experienced the power of analog newsletters while reading _The Gary Halbert Letter_ from the '80s and '90s. Then, I learned it was <u>still</u> a viable business model after listening to Russell Brunson on that fateful day in Tecolote Canyon when he told me about Ben Settle.

The analog monthly newsletter works so well because _recurring revenue_ is built into it. It enables you to earn six figures by writing one thing a month.

However... as I observed the landscape of analog newsletter publishers, I noticed a few shortcomings. Many of them were <u>not</u> selling it properly. For instance, one company was trying to sell its analog monthly newsletter by getting people to subscribe immediately (without a trial). Another was trying to sell theirs by giving away a digital copy of it first. From my own tests (totaling over 100 A/B tests), I knew the shortcomings of this approach.

This led me to <u>the</u> big idea. I asked myself the following question:

What If I Combined <u>All Three</u> Requirements Into <u>One</u> Thing?

That is, what if I combined all three of these components: 1) a **Funnel**, 2) an **Analog Knowledge Tripwire**, and 3) an **Analog Monthly Newsletter**. Combining all three made perfect sense. After all, I knew how critical all three were. It didn't take much deliberation. I soon combined all three into one funnel, and I named it...

The Analog Knowledge Funnel[2]
("The AK Funnel")

---

[2] (The one funnel to rule them all, the one funnel to find them, the one funnel to bring them all, and in the darkness bind them.)

1. Analog Book Page 2. Analog Newsletter Upsell 3. Thank You Page

(Analog Knowledge Tripwire)

From here on, I'll refer to the **Analog Knowledge Funnel** as an "AK Funnel" (for brevity). An AK Funnel is deceptively simple. It took me over a decade to discover it. I had to learn the expensive way (by doing things myself and failing). Now that I had understood the mechanics of this model, I believed I had the ultimate answer to making a fantastic living from my knowledge work. With the AK Funnel, I believed the neo-intellectual life was around the corner. Soon, I'd be able to make six figures by writing one thing a month.

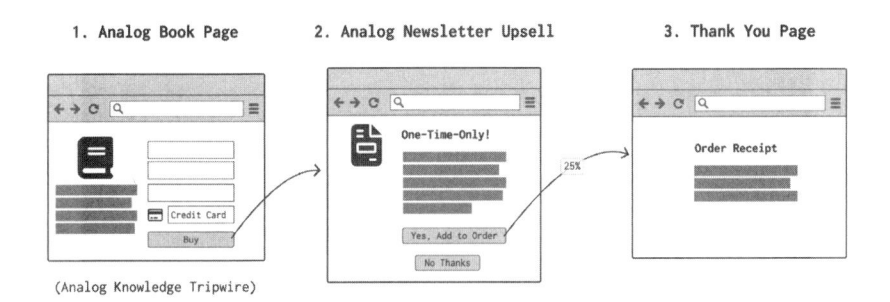

Now that you understand the three components of the AK Funnel, the next part of this journey details putting it into action. Get ready, you're in for a wild ride.

{ Part 4 }
Action

Chapter Seventeen

The Teeniest, Tiniest Niche Ever?

At this time, I had become intrigued by the teeniest, tiniest niche imaginable—something called...

"Zettelkasten"

Zettelkasten is the German word for "notebox." (*Zettel* means "note" and *kasten* means "box.") Zettelkasten refers to a notebox system devised by Niklas Luhmann, a German sociologist. Luhmann wrote over seventy books and six hundred academic papers during his career. This is an astonishing amount of output. As a result, his Zettelkasten system became quite intriguing for those interested in becoming prolific readers, writers, and researchers.

As I researched what people were teaching about Zettelkasten, I discovered something quite unsettling...

Most People Didn't Understand How It _Really_ Worked!

Legions of online "Zettelkasten experts" were trying to retrofit Zettelkasten for the digital age. They were telling people, "Analog notecards aren't important. The important thing is that you *link* your notes together." This was flat-out wrong.

I had spent hours studying the _real_ archives of Niklas Luhmann's Zettelkasten. I reverse-engineered how everything worked. I learned a lot of things that most people were unaware of. As such, I saw an opportunity and decided...

"I Will Write a Book Teaching How Zettelkasten _Really_ Works!"

In doing so, I would shatter all the *conventional* beliefs about the field.[1] I decided to title my book, *Antinet Zettelkasten*.

Given my new discovery of the AK Funnel, I decided to put it to the test.

---

1 Pay attention to this sentence—specifically, the concept of "conventional." This is a critical area that is necessary for success. It's something I first introduced to my readers in Issue No. 5 of my analog newsletter, *The Scott Scheper Letter*. It relates to a concept I teach called "UTSM." The "U" in UTSM stands for "Unconventional." In order to create a bestselling book, it must be unconventional. This is something I won't be able to cover in depth right now. Just know—it's intentionally used here.

Here was my plan: I would write my *Antinet Zettelkasten* book, and then launch it using the AK Funnel.

I thought to myself, **"*If I could make a six-figure living from an AK Funnel—in the teeniest, tiniest niche imaginable—then imagine how powerful it could be in a normal-sized niche?*"**[2]

With this question in mind, I began implementing the details of this plan.

First, I would create an **Analog Book Page**. I would create a page that sold my *Antinet Zettelkasten* book. It would act as my tripwire. I would send first-time visitors to this page so that they could purchase my book. In doing so, I would collect their name, email, and other information. That way, I could begin having a direct relationship with my customers (unlike the Kindle publishing model).

Second, immediately after people purchased my book, I would offer them my *Analog Monthly Newsletter*. As an ode to *The Gary Halbert Letter*, I decided to carry forth his tradition. I decided to use a similar layout and type-

---

[2] Some readers may wonder whether the AK Funnel only works because the Antinet Zettelkasten book espouses the importance of analog. However, this is not what I've found in my tests. Any book in any niche works with an AK Funnel.

face. I named my newsletter, *The Scott Scheper Letter*.

After this, I dug up several old salesletters that Gary Halbert had written. I set aside the ones that promoted analog monthly newsletters. As I studied them, I noticed several <u>critical techniques</u> most people overlooked. I spent a month reverse-engineering these salesletters, and in doing so, **I uncovered <u>eight</u> critical factors that were used across all of them.**

Gary Halbert made the decision to sign up for his analog monthly newsletter <u>irresistible</u>. He did this by implementing the eight critical factors. He also introduced things that would ensure people stayed subscribed for a very, <u>very</u> long time. It became clear that...

If You Miss <u>Even One</u> of These Eight Critical Factors, This Entire Model Could Fail

Therefore, I wrote a sales letter for my *Analog Newsletter Upsell*. It strung together <u>all eight</u> critical factors. After I finished building my AK Funnel, it looked like this:

My AK Funnel

My AK Funnel consisted of only three web pages. Building the website was fairly

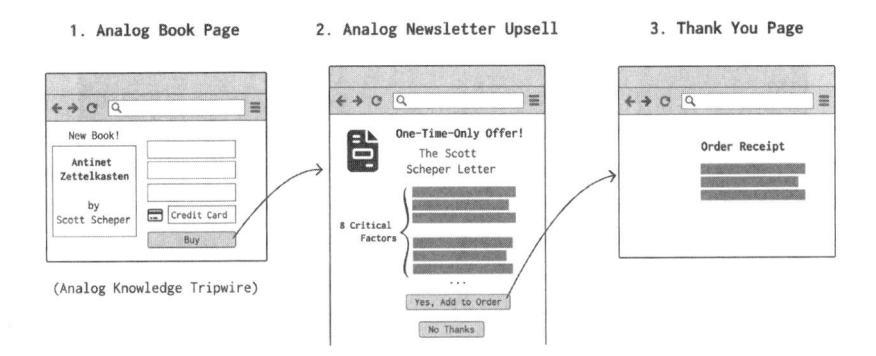

1. Analog Book Page 2. Analog Newsletter Upsell 3. Thank You Page

[Figure: Three browser mockups showing the funnel flow — "New Book! Antinet Zettelkasten by Scott Scheper" with Credit Card / Buy (Analog Knowledge Tripwire) → "One-Time-Only Offer! The Scott Scheper Letter, 8 Critical Factors, Yes, Add to Order / No Thanks" → "Order Receipt"]

straightforward. However, I was using a different software platform than the one I currently use today. Therefore, I had to glue together a bunch of different services and pay a web developer $2,500. Today, creating an AK Funnel takes a few clicks and I don't need a developer.

Next, I embarked on the task of writing the book itself. I didn't work on the book every day. I took breaks and went on some side quests. Overall, I enjoyed the process of writing *Antinet Zettelkasten*. I treated it as my "craft." I wrote the first draft using only pen and notecards.[3] When you set aside an hour a day, it's amazing how fast you can get a book done.[4]

---

3   Just like I wrote the book you're reading right now.

4   In case you're wondering, I've found that a book should be at least 64 pages. Why? Because it <u>feels</u> like an actual book when held. Any less is a bit too thin. I call

I finished writing the book. Next, I turned my attention to finding a printing provider. I was looking for a provider who would handle all the printing, storage, shipping, and fulfillment. (I didn't want my garage filled with 1,000 books.) I didn't want to worry about shipping. (Heck, to this day, I don't know how to ship a book, and I've sold 10,000+ books.) I simply wanted the ease of fulfillment that Amazon provides—I wanted someone to take care of <u>everything</u>.

After scouring the earth—and speaking with dozens of printing presses—I found two of the best providers and partnered with them.

The first printing partner specialized in **analog books**. Their books were of better quality than Amazon's and they cost less![5] In addition, my printing partner could do either *bulk printing* or *print-on-demand printing*. This meant, I didn't have to spend thousands of dollars up front. I could just pay to print one book at a time as orders came in.

---

this the "When I'm 64 Rule." (Like the song by The Beatles.) Write until your book is 64 (at the very least).

5   On Amazon KDP, my book cost $46 to print. With my print partner, it costs only $5.99 to print. (My book was 594 pages. Meaning, it costs more than most books.)

The second printing partner specialized in *analog newsletters*. They were one of the best in the world. Several other analog publishers had been secretly using them for decades.

I then secured deals with each printing partner.[6] I then hired a software developer to connect their APIs to my website's backend.[7] After figuring out these logistics, everything was finished. My AK Funnel was complete. I had everything in place to launch. I was ready!

You now understand the process of building an AK Funnel. I've shown you how I went about building mine. It wasn't easy, but it wasn't impossible either. The good news is that it's an order of magnitude easier today. You no longer have to worry about complex technical integrations or sourcing your own printing partners.

However, the best part of building an AK Funnel is the anticipation of **launch**! That is what I'll detail next.

---

6 I negotiated rates with each partner that are lower than what anyone else gets with them.

7 The software platform I use today handles all of this automatically. I'm telling you this because I don't want to scare you with how complex this sounds!

Chapter Eighteen

No Thanks, Hawaii

As I approached launch week, I was feeling optimistic. I felt like I had learned my lesson from my previous book launch (the one from a decade prior). The failure of doing only $135.27 in royalties was now a distant memory. That was the Kindle publishing model, I told myself. With the AK Funnel, I was confident the neo-intellectual life was around the corner.

It's worth noting what was going on in my personal life at the time...

Without veering _too_ far off track, I will say this: At that time, I was in a relationship with someone who was _not_ the best person in the world for me. She had a lot of insecurities (aka "jealousy issues") stemming from Mommy and Daddy). I'm talking about my ex. She _thrived_ in the department of passive-aggressiveness (she was studying to become a psychologist). It also didn't help that she was *very* pessimistic about my book.

It was two weeks before I was set to launch my book. I got home one evening and she told me her mom and stepdad had invited us to Hawaii. "I realize it would be during your launch week," she said, "but I *really* want to go." She proceeded to share how we'd have to pay our own way. (Meaning *I* would have to pay our own way.) This wasn't a problem. The problem was *timing*.

I explained to my (now ex) how a *lot* was riding on my book launch. I reminded her I'd been working on it all year (even before I had met her). During launch week, I wanted to be in my office—on a reliable internet connection—not on an island in the Pacific. (I had lived on an island before and I knew the realities of island life.)

Anyway—let's just say... she didn't handle it well. "You *always* put your work above me!" She stormed out of our house and got into her car and drove to her mom's house.

I thought she'd cool down after awhile, but... she didn't. She came back that night and announced she'd be going to Hawaii without me. "I'll be paying for everything myself," she said. (My ex hadn't held a stable job in several years and didn't have much in savings.)

The manner with which my ex blew up at me put a damper on my mood. I sensed our relationship was coming to an end. The good news was that I'd have freedom during launch week, at least! She'd be in Hawaii, which meant I could now focus without having my ex (and her pessimism) around.

I set my book's launch date for Friday, December 9th. This meant I would have all week to test my AK Funnel. I could test various credit cards, settings, and other details, allowing me to fix any last-minute bugs.

I spent Monday testing my AK Funnel. Everything was working perfectly. This meant I had four days at my disposal before launch day. What should I do with all my time? It didn't feel right just sitting around, doing nothing—after all, I had turned down a trip to Hawaii (which sent my ex into a tailspin). I felt compelled to be productive with this spare time. Soon, I felt myself getting lured back into the idea of digital publishing. I remember thinking, I have my book files done. They're just sitting here. Why not just upload them to Amazon's Kindle Platform? It couldn't hurt.

I spent the next few minutes rationalizing this thought. I estimated I could earn an additional $3,000 by publishing my book on Kindle. I figured it would complement the revenue generated by my AK Funnel.

With this in mind, I logged back into the platform that had caused me so much turmoil a decade earlier—Kindle Direct Publishing. I then entered information about my book and uploaded its cover file. It couldn't hurt, I told myself.

In the months leading up to my book launch, I started building an **email list**. I knew I would be launching my book using an AK Funnel. Therefore, I wanted a way to notify people when my book launched.

At this point, you may be wondering...

How Do You Build an Email List?

For me, building an email list was quite simple. However, I'd like to first offer a disclaimer: You should not wait until you have an email list to begin building your AK Funnel. You should build your email list *while* you're working on your AK Funnel. Doing so allows you to tease your audience about your forthcoming book. That way, when your book launches, you'll have a list of people <u>anxiously awaiting</u> your book.

I built my email list by posting videos on YouTube. I simply taught people how an analog Zettelkasten works.[1] In the description below the video, I included a link to my website. On the page, I gave away a free PDF guide on Zettelkasten in exchange for their email address. I did this in a <u>very</u> specific way. As a result, I had 1,100 people on my email list by the time launch day arrived, and—before I knew it...

Launch Day Had Arrived!

It was Friday, December 9th. I did not sleep much the previous night. A lot was riding on the launch of my book. I decided to launch it at noon.

At 12:00 p.m. sharp, I sent out an email with a link to my AK Funnel. I monitored the purchases and everything seemed to be working! Orders were succeeding and all of the transac-

---

[1] There are two types of YouTube videos I find to perform well for knowledge creators: (1) hard-teaching videos, and (2) interview-style videos. This is something I detailed in Issue No. 2 of *The Scott Scheper Letter*. In my case, I opted for the first type (hard teaching).

tions were posting to my print partner's backend. Everything was running smoothly.

By 4 o'clock that afternoon, I was tired. I decided to reward myself by heading home early to relax. I ordered takeout and plopped down on my couch. I then began to watch my favorite show, The Mandalorian.[2] My two cats curled up next to me.

I went to bed early that night. I decided I would look at my stats the following morning when orders had finished coming in. I had a feeling things were looking good. I remember thinking, tomorrow, the neo-intellectual life finally begins.

---

2 It was my favorite show, until Disney ruined it in Season 3 (like they do to all shows).

Chapter Nineteen

Engulfed by a Bear

The next morning, I found myself in a pit of despair. It was 6:30 a.m. and I was laying on my downstairs couch. Draped over me was a <u>very</u> heavy bearskin blanket. Resting on my stomach was my beast of a cat, a brown ragdoll named "Mr. Brodus." On the floor next to me was my phone. It was laying where I had thrown it.

I Didn't Feel Like Moving

Fifteen minutes earlier, I had woken up. At that point, I was in a good mood. I grabbed my phone, opened the Amazon app, and searched "Antinet Zettelkasten." It was the #1 bestselling book in two categories! ("Study Skills" and "Writing Skills.")

Here's a screenshot:

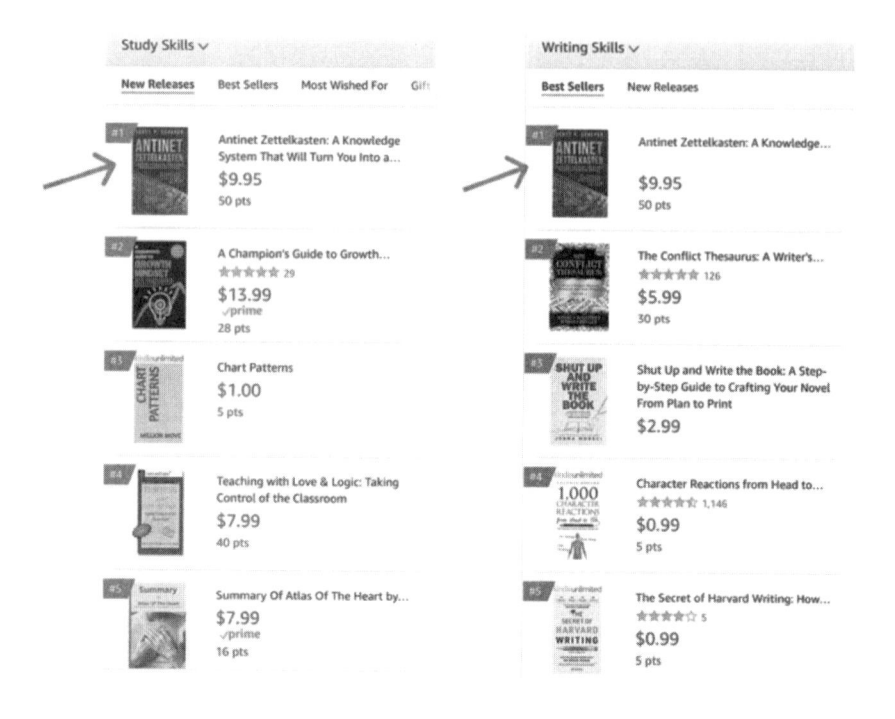

I figured this would mean my royalties on Amazon would far surpass my estimate of $3,000 dollars! I logged into Kindle Direct Publishing. I then checked my royalties. This can't be correct, I thought. I refreshed the page and checked an FAQ. The stats were correct. They were up to date. Amazon reported I had made...

Only $31.64 in Royalties!

This can't be! The feeling I had experienced ten years earlier once again emerged. I started to wonder whether I had once again wasted a year of my life.

I went downstairs and threw myself on my couch. I pulled the heavy bearskin blanket over me and sighed to myself, God dammit!

Then, customer reviews started coming in on Amazon. I refreshed the page and saw several five-star reviews... I then saw my first one-star review, and then another, and another. These were from people who were firmly committed to digital notetaking. (Apps like *Obsidian*, *Notion*, and *Evernote*.)[1] It turns out, they hated what I had to say. You see, I had derided the use of digital tools. In my book, I used research studies and empirical examples to back my arguments for the power of analog—but it didn't matter. They had already committed to digital Zettelkasten. Once beliefs are formed, they're difficult to change. I was telling them they were wrong. As such, I attracted a lot of haters.

My book is 594 pages, I recall myself thinking. How could all these one-star reviewers have finished the book already? The answer is:

---

1 Because such tools use bubble graphs to visualize notes, and—because most users of said tools are obsessed with the bubble graph views—I refer to these people as "Bubble Graph Bois."

they hadn't! The book was published for less than a day. I was getting crushed by trolls with an axe to grind. As I perused the reviews, I realized something. Even the most level-headed reader would have a difficult time parsing out the troll reviews. As a result, most people would be scared away from purchasing my book—a book I had spent almost a year working on!

At this point, I felt the damage was done. I had shot myself in the foot yet again—thanks to digital publishing. I was disappointed with myself.

I threw my phone to the floor. I was sad, but I also knew there was still hope. My AK Funnel was my main focus, after all. Still, it deflated me to see how poorly my Kindle royalties were. They were _way_ lower than expected. I had a _lot_ riding on this book. I was mentally tired, and my body ached. I remember thinking how it felt like I had been hit by a truck. Life was kicking my ass.

My dream of making six figures as an independent writer seemed to be nearing death. Whenever I was asked what I did for a living, I had even begun to tell people, "I'm a writer." Yet, with how things were looking, this wasn't in my future. I'd have to go back to marketing for #HustleCulture startups.

While these thoughts were racing through my mind, I opened my eyes. There, staring back at me, was my ragdoll cat, Mr. Brodus. He gave me his typical "dickish" glare. He looked annoyed with me. If he could speak, he'd be saying...

"Get up and stop being such a pussy, Scott!"

"You're right, Brodus," I said. I got off the couch. I lifted the heavy bearskin blanket off me. It fell to the floor. I picked up my phone and walked into my downstairs office.

In my office was my laptop. I needed it to check the stats of my AK Funnel. I opened my laptop and navigated to the analytics dashboard. It displayed my revenue. What I saw next would change the course of my life. Forever.

Chapter Twenty

Finally

"**T**hirteen-thousand, four-hundred, eighty-two dollars and seven cents!" I said this aloud as I looked at my stats in disbelief. I double-checked, and I had gotten it right:

$13,482.07 in Revenue!

This was from the previous day (Friday, December 9th). I took a screenshot:

Gross volume ⓘ +∞

$13,482.07 $0.00 previous period

$8,614.05

$0.00
Dec 1, 2022, 12:00 AM   Dec 9, 2022, 11:00 PM

View more   Updated 5:17 PM

As elated as I was (and don't get me wrong, I was <u>very</u> elated), I was more elated about something else. While my book revenue validated my audience's interest in Zettelkasten, I knew that book sales were only one-time transactions. It's not where the money is. I couldn't achieve the neo-intellectual life on book sales alone. What got me <u>really</u> excited was what I saw next.

I checked the stats of my Analog Newsletter Upsell Page. **Out of 462 people who purchased my book, 201 subscribed to my analog monthly newsletter!** My subscription price was $48 per month. Starting the following month, I would begin making...

$9,648 Per Month in Recurring Revenue!

This comes out to $115,776 per year! All I had to do from thereon was write one thing a month. I had to simply focus on delivering value to my readers. If I did, I'd be on my way to making six figures writing one thing a month.

While the economics of the AK Funnel were fantastic, something else was just as rewarding. I now had...

A Tribe of Readers I Could Serve Every Single Month!

I opened up my email and found dozens of messages. They were from people who were thanking me. In their words, they were "truly grateful" for my book. For instance, I received this message from an entrepreneur from Manchester, Connecticut: "I was hilariously anxious about getting a copy of your book. So excited for you and to get the tome in my hands!"

What was even more fulfilling was that I now had 201 people in my community—which reminds me—one of the eight critical factors for having success with an analog newsletter is...

Creating a Community!

By including a community with your newsletter, you will increase the average lifespan of your subscribers. As such, you'll build a loyal tribe of people who will become life-long readers of yours.[1]

As I reflect on things, I realize how incredible the AK Funnel _really_ was. It gave me three things:

---

[1] The best part is that your community won't require much work or effort to manage! Because you have an analog newsletter, you can position the community where it's not expected of you to respond to any post. (You don't need to police the forum.) Ask any of the people in my community, they'll tell you how "hands-off" I am. However, it's still important to create a community so that other members who like to connect have an outlet to do so.

1. **Security**. For the first time in my life, I had a business model that allowed me to make a living as an independent writer. **Even better, I could make six figures writing one thing a month!**

2. **Control**. The AK Funnel gave me complete control over my time. I didn't have to post hundreds of things a day like typical hustle-culture bros. I simply needed to write one thing a month.

3. **Connection**. I now had a tiny tribe of readers. They were my true fans. During that year, I had spent a lot of time in isolation. (Writing is a lonely endeavor.) It was nice to have a social outlet where I could connect with people who were passionate about the same things I was.

All three of these things were now a part of my life thanks to the AK Funnel.

At this point, you have witnessed the life-changing implications of the AK Funnel and seen how its economics work (compared with the digital publishing model).

At that moment in my life, I was very happy with how things were going. I could have continued along quietly. I could have kept the concept of the AK Funnel to myself. However, I began to explore a whole different direction. That's what I'll share with you in the final part of this book. Get ready. It's about to get even more exciting.

{ Part 5 }
Rebirth

Chapter Twenty-One

To Teach, or Not To Teach

Over the following months, my revenue kept growing. The best part? It didn't take much effort. I didn't have to rely on getting new customers. Why did my business grow? Because of a factor I mentioned earlier...

The Miracle of <u>Compounding</u>!

My revenue *compounded* thanks to my analog monthly newsletter. The subscribers I already acquired stuck around, and new book purchasers added more subscribers every single day. Soon, I was earning over $20,000 per month!

Here's a screenshot:

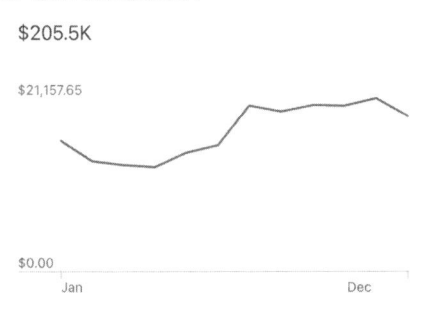

$205.5K

$21,157.65

$0.00

Jan   Dec

Given how much the AK Funnel had changed my life, I started wondering how feasible it would be to teach it to others. I had a lot of people in my community who would _love_ to make a living as an independent writer. Yet, they were left with Amazon KDP as their only option. They knew of no other strategy. So... I began to wonder...

How Hard Would It Be to Teach This Business Model to Others?

As I explored this question, it became apparent that there would be some _serious_ challenges. I came up with a list of three major challenges:

Challenge #1: Technical Obstacles

The "software stack" I was using wasn't simple.[1] I relied on many different platforms. I duct-taped them together with custom webhooks, API integrations, and custom JavaScript (not to mention a few backend services written in Python).

If I were to teach others how to create an AK Funnel, it would be _very_ challenging. For instance, my AK Funnel ran on ClickFunnels.

---

[1] "Software stack" is a phrase nerds use to describe the various technologies they use.

However, because ClickFunnels lacked some basic features, I was forced to purchase a third-party add-on called *CF Pro Tools*. Because this integration relied on embedding JavaScript on the page (and setting certain global variables), and because new ClickFunnels updates would frequently break things, my technical infrastructure was <u>never</u> stable. As a result, I found myself fixing things every other month.

I had expected to just "set it and forget it" (meaning, I expected to create my AK Funnel one time and never touch it again). In reality, I found things breaking regularly for no reason! This made me wonder...

How Could I Expect to Teach Others the AK Funnel If It Needed a "Bug Fix" Every Month?!

Also, there was the website piece. I had the typical web pages (Home Page, Terms of Service, Privacy Policy, etc.). To build it, I used a static-site generator. It was powered by *Amazon Web Services* (S3, CloudFront, and Route 53). In order to make changes to the website, I had to use *Github*, *Microsoft VS Code*, and *Netlify*. Teaching people how to use these things would be a challenge, as well.

In order to power my community, I had to integrate it with my email platform (I was using *Drip* at the time). I then had to integrate that with ClickFunnels. Sound fun? It gets better. This email integration would break whenever there were more than two purchases in a certain timeframe.

In order to post transactions to my printing partners, I had to hire a software development firm. They set up custom webhooks in ClickFunnels (which were also prone to bugs).

In order to generate a mailing list for my analog monthly newsletter (i.e., physical mailing addresses), guess what I had to do? ClickFunnels didn't have this feature. Therefore, I had to pay for an expensive service called *Zapier*. It then posted the data needed from ClickFunnels to Google Sheets. (Surprise, surprise—this was <u>also</u> prone to bugs!)

In order to run this business, I used a whole barrage of other services: a calendar system, a CRM, a pipeline system, Kanban board, invoicing, text messages (for abandoned carts), and on, and on. My expenses grew to be unwieldy. I was literally experiencing death by subscriptions!

As you can gather, there was <u>a lot</u> more complexity involved than what you would expect.

There was no way people could figure this stuff out on their own. Even if they could, would they really want a fragile system prone to bugs? Of course not.

On top of this, there were a lot of nuances many people would overlook. For instance, sequencing email autoresponders properly. There were <u>many</u> small details critical to success.

If I wanted to teach people how to implement all of these technical integrations, it would take months. I'd have to walk them through everything—from account setup, to API integrations, and beyond.

Could I Teach People How to Navigate These Technical Hurdles?

Heck no! Even if it were technically possible, it wouldn't adequately serve them. This was a non-starter for me. But as bad as the technical challenges were, there was another challenge even greater...

Challenge #2: Big Picture Strategy

In order to succeed, a person needed to understand the strategy behind AK Funnels. This wasn't a problem—in fact, by now you already know the strategy behind AK Funnels. However, what's even more important are the other "big picture strategy" items.

For instance, many people don't know what they want to write about. In other words, they need help finding their niche. And for those who know their niche, most of them don't have a clear way of expressing it. Furthermore, many people don't know what it takes to create a bestselling book. They don't know the formula for consistently creating books that sell. I'd have to help them with all of this. Otherwise, they'd be wasting time on a book that was destined to fail.

Figuring these things out would be very difficult for people. They'd have to fail a few times before learning what makes a book sell. In my case, I had learned the hard way. I had created a set of frameworks for creating bestselling books. I could write about these frameworks, however—without my guidance—there was a significant risk of failure.

These were just a few of the big-picture strategy items critical for success. There were others, as well. Which brings me to the third challenge I foresaw...

Challenge #3: The Devilish Details

There were many details involved in building

an AK Funnel—all of which were <u>critical</u> to having success. I had put an inordinate amount of thought into the tiniest of details. **If a person misses just <u>one</u> of these elements, there was no way I could guarantee their success with an AK Funnel.**

Here are just three examples of devilish details: First, you must set up your autoresponder emails in a certain way. Once you do this, you'll retain your subscribers for a <u>much longer</u> period of time.

Second, on the Analog Newsletter Upsell Page, there is a critical way in which I "position" my analog monthly newsletter. (It's not an accident that 44% of the people who buy my book say yes to my analog monthly newsletter.)

The third devilish detail is the most insidious. One easy way you can fail in this journey is through *credit card disputes*. If you try and get "too sneaky" with how you implement your AK Funnel, you're setting yourself up for failure. Why? Because you'll encounter credit card disputes. Even if less than 1% of charges are disputed, your entire business could get shut down overnight.

How Do You Avoid Your Entire Business Being Shut Down Over Night?

Now you're starting to ask the important questions!

These <u>are</u> <u>just</u> <u>three</u> "devil details." However, there are dozens of others. This led me to wonder whether it was even possible to train people in all of these intricacies.

At this point, I'll recap what the problem was...

My goal was to create the neo-intellectual life for myself. That is, I wanted to make a six-figure living through writing.

After failing to achieve this (for over a decade), I had finally succeeded—thanks to the AK Funnel.

I started wondering if I could help others who wanted the same type of lifestyle, and—in contemplating this—I knew there would be three major problems: (1) **The Technical Obstacles**, (2) **The Big Picture Strategy**, and (3) **The Devilish Details**.

Yet, the question remained...

How Do I Help People Overcome These Three Challenges So That They Can Succeed With The Analog Knowledge Funnel?

One option was to give up the idea of teaching AK Funnels. I seriously contemplated this route.[2] However, I decided to pursue a mission bigger than myself. I decided my mission is to create an army of independent writers, researchers, and entrepreneurs. By pursuing this mission, I knew I could have a much bigger impact—while still enjoying the neo-intellectual life.

I dedicated the rest of the year to solving the three challenges. If I could figure out how to solve them, I'd be able to help others have success with AK Funnels.

It ended up taking most of the year. However, one by one, I solved each challenge—starting with the technical challenge. Which brings me to...

The One Platform to Rule Them All

Teaching people how to glue together ten different software services was not the solution. Therefore, I spent eight months trying

---

2   I thought about just working on my next book idea at the time, a book about the power of excerpting notes by hand (something Gary Halbert termed "neural imprinting.") Writing things out by hand helps you imprint ideas on your mind in a more effective way. This is something every good copywriter knows, yet many people aren't aware of it. For now, this book is just another one I've added to my list of books to write in the future!

to solve this challenge. I had a few false starts. I tried building my own software platform from scratch. It didn't work out. I then discovered a company with over 600 employees who could power the backend infrastructure of what I needed. They would power the funnels, websites, CRM, email platform, and more. Their technology was better than my duct-taped ClickFunnels solution (and more reliable, too).

There was only one problem. It was the default manner in which the software platform was set up. Out of the box, it wasn't built for people like me (independent writers and entrepreneurs). It was built for service businesses—i.e., realtors, agencies, and law firms. I needed a platform that catered specifically to my needs—a solopreneur running an analog knowledge business.

So, here's what I did: I partnered with the company and gutted out all of the "bloatware" I didn't need. I then completely overhauled the frontend interface, and I added all of the features I needed.

I added **Analog Book** functionality to the platform. After you log in, on the left-hand side of the platform, there's a tab labeled "Books." Here's a screenshot:

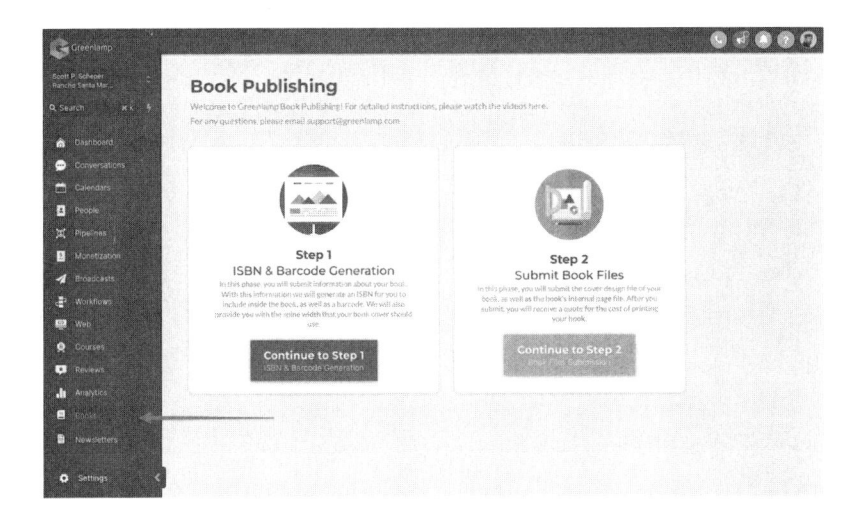

All you have to do is click a few buttons and fill out your book info. After that, you'll be selling, printing, and shipping your book in no time. The process is even simpler than Amazon's KDP Platform.[3] As a result...

You Won't Have to Worry About
Printing and Shipping Your Book, And...
You Keep 100% of The Royalties!

After this, I built *Analog Newsletter* functionality into the platform. After you log in, you simply click the "Newsletters" tab (picture below):

---

3   There are less fields involved compared to Amazon's KDP. Plus, getting a real ISBN is much easier than Amazon's process—and it's free! Amazon assigns their own version of ISBN. There are several drawbacks to this—one being that they can only be sold inside Amazon's ecosystem.

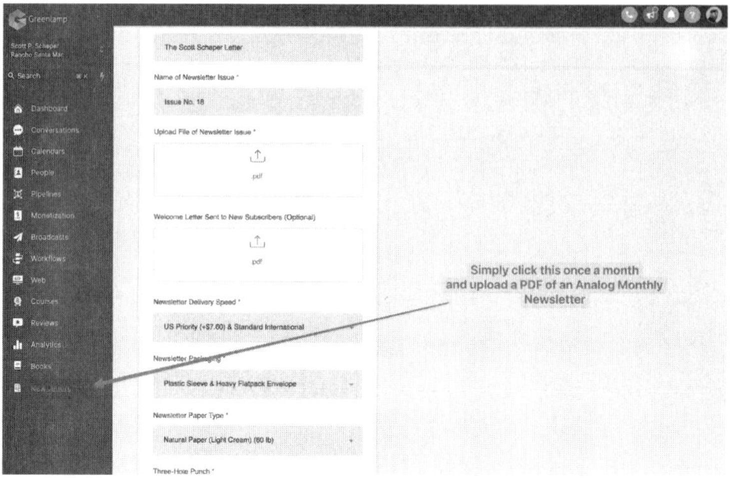
The Scott Schaper Letter
Name of Newsletter Issue *
Issue No. 18
Upload File of Newsletter Issue *
Welcome Letter Sent to New Subscribers (Optional)
Newsletter Delivery Speed *
US Priority (+$7.60) & Standard International
Plastic Sleeve & Heavy Flatpack Envelope
Newsletter Paper Type *
Natural Paper (Light Cream) (60 lb)
Three-Hole Punch *
Simply click this once a month
and upload a PDF of an Analog Monthly
Newsletter

All you have to do is upload a PDF once a month of your newsletter. After that, your newsletter is shipped to people across the globe.

On top of this, I now had the ability to natively create ***AK Funnels***. Here's a screenshot:

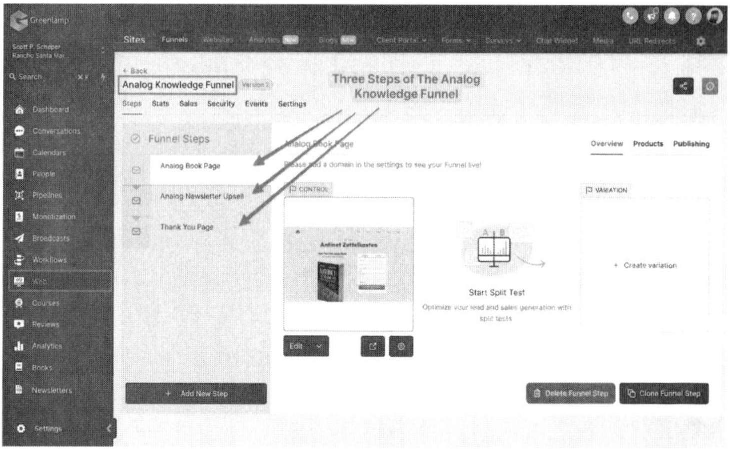
Analog Knowledge Funnel
Three Steps of The Analog
Knowledge Funnel
Funnel Steps
Analog Book Page
Analog Newsletter Upsell
Thank You Page
Overview
Products
Publishing
Start Split Test
Create variation
Add New Step
Delete Funnel Step
Clone Funnel Step

All I had to do was simply click the "Web" tab and select "Funnels." From there, I could build an AK Funnel by simply dragging and dropping the web elements I needed.

There are other features built into the platform, as well (emails, autoresponders, websites, blog, analytics, courses, communities, calendars, CRM, and more). As a result, instead of logging into ten different services, I only needed one platform to power everything. I now had...

One Platform To Rule Them All!

I decided to name the platform: **Greenlamp** (because I love green banker desk lamps—I have three of them in my office). To me, it symbolizes old-school hard work. Whenever I sit down to write, I have a ritual. I dim the lights, and then I flick on my green desk lamp. Now—whenever I'm ready to <u>distribute</u> my writing online— I turn on my laptop and flick on *Greenlamp*!

With the creation of *Greenlamp*, I solved the technical challenge of analog publishing. *Greenlamp* made it simple to build AK Funnels. Now, I could help people succeed <u>without</u> having to glue fifteen different software services together. I was one step closer to creating an army of independent writers, researchers, and entrepreneurs.

Now that I had *Greenlamp*, the next step was putting it to the test. That's what I'll show you in the next chapter.

Chapter Twenty-Two

Push-Button Simple

Now that I had *Greenlamp*, I decided to put it to the test. I decided to see how "push-button simple" it would be to create an AK Funnel.[1] Here's what I did...

At that point, I had a 63-page PDF guide I had written. It was titled *Getting Started with an Antinet Zettelkasten*. In order to download the guide, people had to enter their email addresses. From there, I'd automatically email customers a link to the PDF.[2] While it was nice to see my email list grow, I ended up with a lot of "freebie seekers." I asked myself,

---

1 Notice how I use the term "push-button simple" and not "push-button easy." Why is that? It's because I don't think anything is "easy." If you do things right, then it should be "hard." Why? Because anything "easy" is also easy to replicate (which brings copycats). You don't want to strive for things to be easy; you want to strive for things to be simple (but hard).

2 Many marketers refer to this as a "Lead Magnet."

what's better than an email list of freebie seekers? The answer was simple...

An Email List of <u>Actual</u> <u>Paying</u> <u>Customers</u>!

With this in mind, I decided to remove the 63-page free PDF from my website. Then, I logged into *Greenlamp* and uploaded the PDF to the "Books" tab. A few days later, the book was printed and my AK Funnel was built. I then sent out an email announcing the 63-page PDF guide was now available to purchase in <u>analog</u> form. It ended up helping me generate...

$7,912.87 in Revenue That Week!

Gross volume ⓘ

$7,912.87

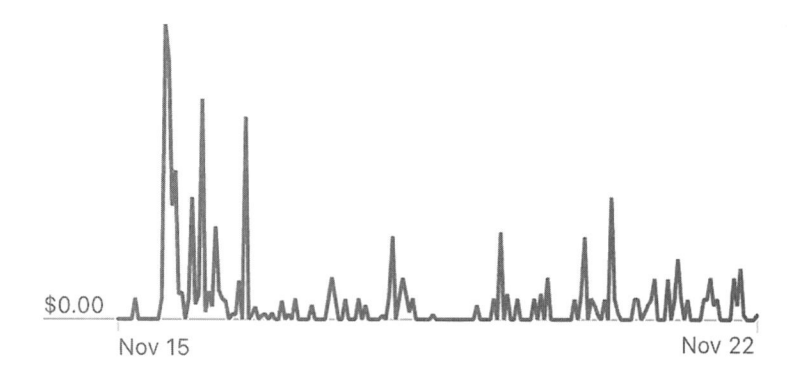

Nov 15 — Nov 22

The best part was that I acquired thirty-two additional subscribers for my analog monthly newsletter. Even if only 80% of them stay subscribed, it comes out to **an additional $23,390.64 in revenue I'd be collecting that year!**[3]

These results were phenomenal. It proved how straightforward it is to build a successful AK Funnel. It took me only a few steps and I did everything from one platform—*Greenlamp*!

This proved to me that others could build AK Funnels without advanced tech skills. I simply uploaded a PDF to *Greenlamp* and created an AK Funnel with the push of a button. Without sounding *too* sensationalistic...

Creating an AK Funnel Was Now Push-Button Simple!

I had solved the biggest concern I had about teaching others AK Funnels (the *technical challenge*). Yet, there were still two other challenges I had to solve: the **big-picture strategy** and the **devilish details**.

---

3   Here's the math: 32 subscribers x 0.80 = 26 subscribers. The average price of my newsletter during that period was $74.97 (($59.95 + $68.96 + $96) / 3). Thus, (26 subscribers x $74.97) x 12 months = $23,390.64.

In order to solve these problems, I had to get out of my cave and into the field. That's what I'll detail in the next chapter. Keep reading. You're about to learn a lot from a real-life example!

Chapter Twenty-Three

Freedom Writers

I had solved the technical challenge of creating AK Funnels. Great. But I couldn't give people access to *Greenlamp* and expect them to automatically have success. There was the **big-picture strategy challenge** people needed to overcome. Not only would people need to be taught the AK Funnel, they would also need to approach it correctly.

For instance: They'd need to figure out their perfect niche. They'd need to position themselves correctly. They'd need to develop a powerful message and communicate it clearly, and... they'd need to encapsulate all of this into a book that sells like crazy!

I also needed to help people overcome the **devilish details**. I'm talking about things like autoresponder emails, and critical website copy that can make or break their success.

With this in mind, I put my thinking cap on. After three months, I created a master plan. I devised something that would solve both challenges. I decided to launch an *incubator*—something where I could "incubate" people for a short period of time and "hatch them" into successful independent writers. I would teach them all of the frameworks I knew to nail their niche and craft a bestselling book for their dream audience.

On top of this, I would give them access to their own *Greenlamp* account. Then, I would **give them keys to a pre-built AK Funnel.** I'd also build out everything they'd need: Autoresponders, email templates, and more. That way, they'd have all the *devilish details* needed to succeed. I decided to build out all of these critical details into their *Greenlamp* account for them.

I would give them everything needed to create the neo-intellectual life—one of absolute freedom. The path to freedom came through writing. As such, I decided to name my incubator...

Write to Freedom

I spent the majority of that year developing *Write to Freedom*. I wanted everything to be in place for people to have success. At the end of the year, I decided to run a "Freedom Writer" through Write to Freedom.[1] I'm going to tell you about her now:

Hailey René from Houston, Texas

Hailey is a young woman from Houston, Texas. She became a subscriber of my analog newsletter after purchasing my *Antinet Zettelkasten* book. One day, I noticed Hailey had been very active in my community. She was helping people implement the concepts I was teaching in my newsletters.

After chatting with Hailey, two things became apparent: (1) she was smart, and (2) she desired the neo-intellectual life.

Hailey had been taking time off from attending her university. She didn't have a job. Why? Because she didn't want to go back to working for some soul-sucking company. Her real passion, I came to find out, was in the field of personal development—specifically, she was fascinated with the idea of using notecards to develop her life.

I asked Hailey if she would be interested in writing a book about personal development. She

---

[1] "Freedom Writer" is a term I use to refer to those in Write to Freedom.

said yes. I then asked her if she wanted a lifestyle where she could make a living as an independent writer. "How?" she asked me. I detailed the AK Funnel and showed her how all she had to do was write one thing a month. "I'm in," she replied.

With this, I admitted Hailey into *Write to Freedom*. She was my first Freedom Writer. I created short videos that I asked Hailey to watch. Each video came with a small, detailed task for her to carry out. She watched all of the videos and began working on her AK Funnel. I also had her watch videos that introduced frameworks for shaping her book idea. I then worked with her on coming up with a killer book title and subtitle. I also showed her my process for writing books—the analog way. She began writing her book. The title she settled on was *Soul Cards: A Powerful Technique for Getting to Know Yourself Deeply*.

After two months, she finished writing her book. We then turned our attention to working on the *devilish details*. I cloned everything she needed into her *Greenlamp* account. I simply had her customize the text. (For instance, in the receipt emails she replaced my book title with her own.) Shortly thereafter, she launched her AK Funnel. Here are her results...

Greenlamp	Page Views		Opt-Ins				Sales		
	All	Uni...	All	Rate	Orders	Rate	Quantity	Amount	Avg. c...
> ✉ Analog Book Page	983	771	202	26.20%	139	18.03%	153	$1377.00	$9.91
> ✉ Analog Newsletter Upsell	169	142	-	-	38	26.76%	38	$570.00	$15.00
> ✉ Thank You Page	141	107	-	-	-	-	-	-	-

Previous

Hailey had 771 people visit her website. Of those who visited, 18.03% of people ordered her book (this is great!) This comes out to 139 people in total who ordered Hailey's book.

Now... here's where things <u>really</u> start to get fun. Out of the 139 book purchasers, 38 of them said yes to a trial of Hailey's analog monthly newsletter. Hailey charges $15 for the first month of the trial. This covers the cost of printing and shipping the newsletter (which usually costs around $11 per newsletter, depending on page length). After thirty days, people are enrolled in the regular subscription price of $49 per month.

I've found that roughly 90% of people stay on after the thirty-day trial. That means, Hailey could expect 34 subscribers on her second month. This would come out to $1,666 in revenue starting on month two. Not bad! If we assume a cost per newsletter of $11, that comes out to **$1,292 profit per month!**

Now... the real beauty of this model is that it's *monthly recurring revenue (MRR)*. That means it has the potential to *compound* every month![2] Hailey isn't making six figures—yet—but she's making the type of (semi) passive income most writers wouldn't mind. People who get into Kindle publishing dream of this type of income, but they rarely ever attain it!

Hailey went through *Write to Freedom* and came out the other end with incredible results. She proved that I could solve the other two big problems (*big-picture strategy* and *devilish details*).

After seeing the results of Hailey, I was very excited. My confidence in AK Funnels grew even more. I had solved all three challenges (the *technical challenge*, the *big-picture strategy*, and the *devilish details*). I became confident I could help others attain the neo-intellectual life.

---

[2] I just checked in with Hailey while writing this chapter. It's been six months since she launched. She has been busy and hasn't had the time to promote her book. She's done nothing to promote her book since it launched six months ago. Guess how many subscribers she has now? Answer: 35 subscribers! This means she's doing $1,681 in monthly revenue—and she hardly does anything! She simply writes one analog newsletter a month.

Over the following months, I helped many others launch their own AK Funnels. For instance, Kathleen Spracklen, a 76-year-old retired computer scientist. I helped her launch an AK Funnel for her book *Writing with Emotion*. She generated $1,368.45 in book sales and is now making $1,037.90 per month from her analog monthly newsletter. This was just the beginning! She's now on the journey to $10,000 per month.

After helping Kathleen, I helped two entrepreneurs, Ken Caputo and Stephanie Anne Roy. After years of struggling to gain traction for their online business, I helped them launch a book titled *The Spiral: How to Design a Life That is Self-Sustaining and Momentum-Gaining*. In their first week, they generated $923.51 in book sales and are now making $1,044 per month from their analog monthly newsletter.

I went on to help many others write their books and launch AK Funnels, and they began experiencing tremendous success. **Within my community, you will meet Hailey René, Kathleen Spracklen, Stephanie Anne Roy, Ken Caputo, and many others.**

However, I want to point out something very important—**the first milestone is $1,000 in MRR (monthly recurring revenue).**

Here's why: The hardest part of starting any business is going from $0 to $1,000 in MRR. After you attain this goal, hitting $10,000 MRR becomes comparatively easy. While $1,000 per month in recurring revenue doesn't sound like much, it's nothing to laugh at. It's extremely hard to do. Albeit it's not the end destination, but—before you know it—you will grow to $10,000 per month in recurring revenue. From there, you can grow to $100,000+ per month (just like I have).

It sounds counterintuitive, but—if your goal is to make over $100,000 per month with this model, you do not want to focus on $100,000 per month. Instead, you want to focus on $1,000 per month. From there, you must focus on $10,000 per month, and then—(and only then)—should you focus on $100,000 per month.

I have a module in *Write to Freedom* called "From Six to Seven Figures." It is comprised of six strategies for scaling from six figures to seven figures. It's the very last module for a reason. Why? Because you must master the fundamentals first. Only then should you scale beyond that.

The lesson here is—don't be swayed by the promises out there to "make $500k per month!" That is not what you want to focus on. **What** you want to focus on instead is one thing and one thing only—the first milestone—$1,000 per month in **recurring revenue**.

Before I knew it, I was surrounded by other independent writers who were making a killer living from their analog monthly newsletter. We were all living the neo-intellectual life. The AK Funnel had unlocked this lifestyle. I had entered a new chapter in my journey—in fact, I had become a new person. In the next chapter, I'll tell you what I transformed into.

Chapter Twenty-Four

The Crazy Ones

Six months after launching my AK Funnel, my monthly revenue had <u>compounded</u>. I was earning over $20,000 per month. I was officially living the neo-intellectual life. I had total <u>freedom</u>. I would get to my office whenever I wanted—usually around 11 a.m. (after an unrushed morning spent with my now-wife).[1] After getting to my office, I would spend my days reading, writing, thinking, and taking notes.

One day, I was recording a video for my *Write to Freedom* incubator. I got to a part where I referred to our group as "independent writers, researchers, and entrepreneurs." That's a mouthful, I thought. I guess we could call ourselves "WTFers." (WTF is the acro-

---

1 Yes, after breaking things off with my ex, I moved from San Diego to Orange County. After a few months, I met the love of my life who later became my wife! Don't settle. There's a dream person out there for everyone.

nym for *Write to Freedom* and something else.) That didn't seem fitting either. Then, I had a realization...

We Are Penpreneurs!

Pen refers to the writing instrument, and *preneur* refers to the French term meaning "to take." What's a *penpreneur?* **A penpreneur is someone who <u>takes</u> their <u>pen</u> and writes their way to freedom!** How? By leveraging an Analog Knowledge Funnel! Not through ghostwriting, freelancing, copywriting (or working for an external institution.)[2]

I Am a Penpreneur!

There are other penpreneurs, as well. Hailey René, Kathleen Spracklen, Stephanie Anne Roy, Ken Caputo, Rachel Warmath, Mel Jeffcoat—and many others! We are a rapidly growing group. Lately, there's been a new penpreneur born every week! (i.e., someone who launches their AK Funnel and moves toward a six-figure living writing one thing a month.)

I hold that most writers get into writing because they want to become penpreneurs. They

---

2 In Appendix A of this book, you can view the full "Penpreneur Creed" for more detail on our beliefs.

don't want to do what they end up doing (freelancing, ghostwriting, copywriting, Kindle publishing, and blogging). A penpreneur is different...

**Penpreneurs Are The "Crazy Ones"
Who Actually <u>Wrote</u> Their Way to Freedom!**

It's important to point out how this journey led me not only to the life I wanted, but also to becoming an entirely new person. **I became a penpreneur.** I shed my old self—the self that "hustled" his way to success, and I began to make a killer living writing one thing a month—with just a pen, paper, and my brain.

We've covered a lot in this book. However, it's important to reflect on what has been learned—reason being—you're going to undergo the same transformation. In becoming a penpreneur, you're going to shed your "old self" as you embark on this journey.

In the next chapter, I'm going to recap things and also take you through the updated model of—the neo-intellectual life.

Chapter Twenty-Five

A Look Back

As I write this chapter, my monthly earnings have *compounded* even more.

**I'm Now Earning
Over $290,000 Per <u>Month</u>!**

As I reflect back, it's amazing how far *we've* come.[1] If you recall, I originally set out on this journey more than a decade ago. I was trying to escape my first job (the one I hated). I was commuting two hours a day and desired something more fulfilling. But I still needed to pay the mortgage. My initial goal was to make $6,000 per month. I'm now doing almost fifty times that per month!

Not only did I want to live comfortably, I wanted a life where I wasn't stressed about

---

[1] I say "we've" because, at this point, the penpreneur movement is much bigger than me.

work. I wanted to be fully present while at home (not chained to checking messages on *Slack*). I now have a life where I don't <u>ever</u> feel the need to check my phone.

At the beginning of this book, I told you that you'd have a three-word answer to the question, "*How do you make six figures writing one thing a month?*"

Those three words are:

Analog Knowledge Funnel

Now you know the answer. The AK Funnel enables the lifestyle of a penpreneur. With this business model, I've been able to finally achieve the neo-intellectual life.

Here's what the <u>real</u> neo-intellectual life looks like...

A Look Back / 195

The Neo-Intellectual Life
(Analog Publishing)

You

Spend your days...

―― Inputs ――
- Reading
- Writing
- Thinking
- Taking Notes

You produce...

―― Outputs ――
- Papers
- Books
- Teaching (Optional)

For...

You pay yourself $$$

―― Internal Institution ――
Analog Publishing

Analog Knowledge Funnel

Pays $$$

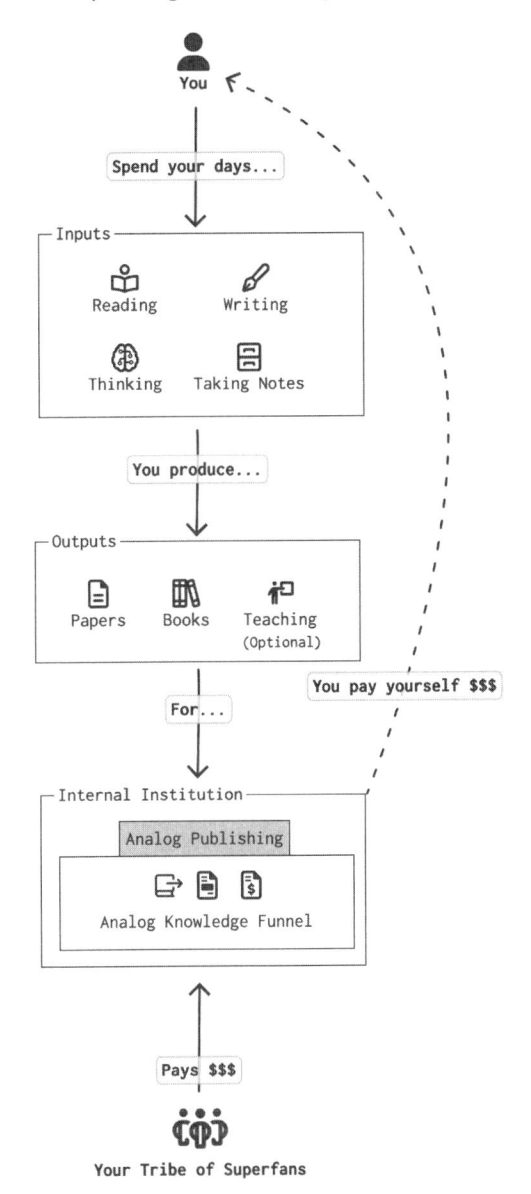

Your Tribe of Superfans

The neo-intellectual life wasn't possible without analog publishing and the AK Funnel. With this model, I'm making over $290,000 per month. More importantly, many others are <u>finally</u> succeeding as analog publishers.

I want you to notice something important. With the neo-intellectual life, you're building an *internal institution*—that is, you're building your <u>own</u> asset that you'll have for the rest of your life. This acts as a profit center that builds your bank account. From there, you can invest these profits which, in turn, creates true <u>wealth</u>.

Wealth is different than money. However, you need money to create wealth. The neo-intellectual life gives you both. **The plain intellectual life gives you a <u>living</u>, whereas the neo-intellectual life gives you a <u>life</u>**. And yet—while the monetary rewards are noteworthy—there's something even more important. That's what I want to share with you next.

Chapter Twenty-Six

Tribe of Superfans

Don't get me wrong. Wealth is great. Freedom is great. But *analog publishing* has unlocked something even more rewarding. You see, by pursuing my passion, I had accumulated a **tribe of superfans**. I had a small group of roughly three hundred people to whom I wrote for every month (and I <u>repelled</u> everyone else who wasn't a fit!) I only attracted my core group of people, and that is precisely what you want to do, as well.

I now get letters every single month in the mail thanking me for what I do. Here's a photo I took:

Once you lean into your passion and write for yourself (and your dream readers), you will begin experiencing the same level of fulfillment.

You'll have hundreds of people thanking you—people who love reading what you write about—and people **you** get to serve every single month. How? It's simple...

Analog Knowledge Creates Deep Emotional Connections

The power of analog knowledge is being discovered from the unlikeliest of sources. Take, for instance, the digital notetaking app, *Evernote*. The founder of *Evernote*, Phil Libin, saw that his sales were declining. Digital notetaking apps were becoming a commodity. Every other month, there was a new notetaking app that stole market share. So, what did Libin do? He made a conscious decision to "take the company in the opposite direction of its virtual roots." Libin created analog knowledge products for *Evernote*. They introduced *Evernote* analog notebooks (through a collaboration with Moleskine). They introduced Post-it notes, desk accessories, pencil holders, and more. According to Evernote's VP of Marketing, customers who purchased these analog knowledge products used the digital app 10% more than they did before.

"People get excited about physical products," he exclaimed. "They get emotionally attached."[1]

The reason I've been able to create such a deep connection with my readers stems precisely from the same source. Thanks to the AK Funnel, not only have my readers been indoctrinated by my analog book, they're <u>re-indoctrinated</u> every month thanks to my analog monthly newsletter.

This is the effect you can unlock with your customers—no matter what industry, niche, or topic. It all comes by way of implementing an Analog Knowledge Funnel. Not only does an AK Funnel yield incredible financial results, it also gives you something money can't buy—the <u>fulfillment</u> of making a life-changing impact **on the types of people you care about.**

Here's an illustration of this: As I was working on the final edits of this book, guess who bought my *Antinet Zettelkasten* book? None other than...

Russell Brunson!

He sent me a text message: "Your funnel/copy are amazing... excited to see your book!!"

---

1 David Sax, *The Revenge of Analog*, 222-3.

I'm telling you this to illustrate that—if you follow your heart, you'll end up attracting the types of readers you dream of serving!

The takeaway is simple: Lean into your passion, embark on this journey, stay focused, and stay persistent. Good things will come, but give yourself time.

The next chapter is the most important chapter in the entire book. You're at a "decision point." I'm going to invite you to make your own decision. You learned the importance of <u>deciding</u> at the end of Chapter 11 (that's when my journey <u>really</u> took off). Now, it's your turn.

Chapter Twenty-Seven

A Look Ahead

I had gone from a broke 9-5'er who failed as an independent writer—to someone who is now making over $290,000 per month. I have become a **penpreneur**. I'm living the neo-intellectual life. More importantly—I'm now creating an army of other penpreneurs!

While making six figures is nice, I got what I really wanted—I now have a tribe of amazing people who share my interests. (We're a group who love reading, writing, learning, and thinking—using analog tools!) Everything I have is thanks to analog publishing—specifically, the Analog Knowledge Funnel.

As I look ahead, here's what I want for you...

**I Want YOU to Be
The Next Chapter
in This Story!**

I want to work with you <u>personally</u>. I want to help you build your AK Funnel. I want to make sure you get the *big-picture strategy* right, as well as the *devilish details*.

What I'm getting at is—I want you to become a penpreneur. How? By joining me in **Write to Freedom**.

If you've read this far, then it's my honor to <u>personally</u> invite you to *Write to Freedom*. From time to time, I have spots open up in *Write to Freedom*. Keep an eye out for any openings. I send emails whenever there's availability.

Until then, I would love to see you around in my community (aka, my "Tribe"). It's free to join, and you've received an invitation after purchasing this book.

I look forward to meeting you someday soon!

                        Warm regards,
                        And always remember,
                        To stay crispy, my friend.

Scott P. Scheper

"A Penpreneur"

Appendix A

Penpreneur Creed

The following creed is for those who wish to become **penpreneurs**. Creeds are traditionally very serious. This one is no different. By reciting this creed, you are shedding your old self and taking on a new life.

This creed is <u>not</u> rooted in a particular religious tradition—it remains mutually exclusive. There are Catholic penpreneurs, Jewish penpreneurs, Muslim penpreneurs, and atheist penpreneurs. A penpreneur strives to better themselves within the arena of everyday life.

On the following pages, you will find the **Penpreneur Creed**. After you read it, I encourage you—if you feel called—to recite this out loud. If you commit to becoming a penpreneur, I promise you—you will unlock the most fulfilling intellectual experience of your life.

[Begin]

I am a penpreneur.

I commit to taking up my pen and writing my way to freedom.

I do not sell my time to external institutions. Nor do I sell my writing in the form of freelancing.

I produce knowledge for my own internal institution, as well as my tribe.

I strive to build a tribe comprised of 1,000 true fans. I stay true to my message, and I am not tempted to "water things down" in hopes of appealing to the masses.

My goal is not to appeal to as many people as possible, but to **repel** as many people as possible!

I spend my days reading, writing, thinking, and taking notes. When I feel like scaling my income, I can opt to teach.

I do not have any social media apps installed on my phone. The only apps I have are for managing content.

In fact, I opt for a "dumb phone" over a "smart phone."

If I participate in the social media channel, I do not <u>consume</u> media, I <u>produce</u> media.

I am present where others are not—in the mailbox, on doorsteps, and in the hands of my dream customers—in the form of **analog knowledge**.

All of my writing starts with pen and paper—whether that be a notecard, legal pad, commonplace book, or other paper-based tool.

I <u>never</u> use ChatGPT or other large language models to do my thinking for me.

I use analog technologies to **develop** knowledge.

I use digital technologies to **distribute** knowledge.

I opt for <u>simplicity</u> over <u>complexity</u>.

I'd rather make $5 million with zero employees than $50 million with 250 employees.

As a penpreneur, I will have something billionaires will never have—enough.

I do not listen to **unstructured information** such as YouTube interviews or podcasts. Such media are advertisements in disguise.

I only listen to **knowledge**. Knowledge is **structured information**, which includes lectures, audiobooks, and courses.

I do not watch television—in fact, when feasible—I opt to rid such devices from my environment.

Instead of television, I opt for evenings spent reading, relaxing, exploring, playing, and conversing.

When I read, I read books in their entirety—without marking up the margins, dog-earing pages, or taking any notes.

I hold my place in books using a bibcard.

After I finish reading a book, I extract only one note from it—the most important piece of knowledge—and I install it into my Antinet Zettelkasten.

In reading, I trust my memory will recall the one piece of knowledge that is truly irresistible after finishing the book.

My Antinet acts as the staging post from which I craft <u>truly</u> <u>original</u> bodies of work.

I create *analog knowledge products*, which include analog books, analog newsletters, and analog courses.

I monetize my intellectual output by way of the *Analog Knowledge Funnel*.

There's no "exit plan" for what I do. I'm building an asset around my <u>own</u> brand, which I'll have for the rest of my life.

I will never sell my analog knowledge business—no matter what the price. I will instead create an asset that generates wealth for the rest of my life.

I adopt a "turtle mindset." That is, I move slowly and deliberately.

I do not divert my mind with any foolish project of growing suddenly rich—for industry and patience alone are the surest means of plenty.

When starting out, my <u>only</u> focus is writing and launching a book using an AK Funnel.

The AK Funnel is the rock upon which everything else is built.

I look at year-over-year growth only.
I stay dogmatically persistent. I do not
quit. I finish what I start. Period.

I embrace doing things the hard way, the
deliberate way, the analog way. This is the
penpreneur way. I know that—in the end—
the penpreneur way is the best way.

I realize there are other
penpreneurs—we are an _actual_ body of
people. We are a network state—
a nation of people scattered all over
the globe who will one day meet up
in a physical location.

The thing bringing us together
is our honest pursuit of the
neo-intellectual life.

I am not perfect. However, I will
commit to following these principles
to the best of my ability.

I am committed to the way.

I am...

A penpreneur.

[End]

If you have taken up this creed and recited it to yourself, welcome! We are a group that is open, curious, and committed to learning. We are not closed, defensive, or committed to being right. As such—if you have taken up this creed, I would love for you to introduce yourself. Please log in to my *tribe* by visiting the following website: **members.scottscheper.com**. After you log in, please post in the main feed and write, *"I am a penpreneur. This is the way."* Then, introduce yourself and share your background.

Glossary

#HustleCultureBro

- <u>Defined</u>: A #HustleCultureBro believes in 5:00 a.m. ice plunges, red light therapy, and push-ups (while tweeting all day, responding to notifications, putting out fires, and working 70+ hours a week). Typically he or she suffers from mommy or daddy issues and will never have enough.

Analog Book Page

- <u>Defined</u>: A web page that acts as the first step in the *AK Funnel*. The Analog Book Page offers a book (at cost of shipping and printing). It is not a profit center, but a "value vehicle" or "loss leader." The Analog Book Page is the best vehicle to use as a *tripwire* for new customers to stumble into your world.

Analog Knowledge Funnel

- <u>Variant Terms</u>: *AK Funnel*, *AKF*
- <u>Defined</u>: A three-page funnel that serves

as the foundation on which one builds the neo-intellectual life. It is the ultimate vehicle of Analog Publishing for making six figures writing one thing a month.

Analog Monthly Newsletter

- Alternate Terms: Analog Newsletter, Physical Monthly Newsletter, Physical Newsletter
- Defined: A piece of knowledge delivered in physical form to a paying subscriber every month. Analog Newsletters are typically 8-24 pages in length. They act as the recurring-revenue engine from which your entire analog publishing business is built from.

Analog Newsletter Upsell Page

- Defined: A web page that comes after the Analog Book Page (usually immediately after). The Analog Newsletter Upsell Page entices the book purchaser with a subscription to the Analog Monthly Newsletter. There are eight critical factors necessary to implement this page in a way that results in a good portion of visitors opting in to the Analog Monthly Newsletter.

Analog Publishing

- Defined: A category of publishers who focus on making their knowledge available in physical form. This includes analog books, analog newspapers, analog monthly newsletters, and more.

Digital Publishing

- Variant Terms: *Mass Digital Publishing, Kindle Publishing, Amazon KDP Publishing*
- Defined: Leveraging Amazon's Kindle Direct Publishing platform to produce books, audiobooks, and even physical books. Although physical books are possible with Amazon KDP, it is not the focus, nor is it the profit center of the platform. *Digital Publishing* is based on the idea of publishing a book and having Amazon's hordes of customers find it automatically.

Neo-Intellectual Life

- Defined: A lifestyle similar to what the Catholic monk Antonin Sertillanges outlined in his book, *The Intellectual Life*. This is a lifestyle where you spend your days reading, thinking, and writing. Except—instead of relying on funding from institutions (academic, religious, or otherwise)—you rely on funding from yourself. This results in ultimate freedom. A life where you get to spend your days doing what you love, without answering to anyone but your readers.

Penpreneur

- <u>Defined</u>: A penpreneur is someone who takes up their pen and writes their way to freedom. A penpreneur makes a living writing for *themselves* (without freelancing, ghostwriting, copywriting, or trading their time for money). Penpreneurs achieve such through building an *Analog Knowledge Funnel*. (For more, see Appendix A: The Penpreneur Creed.)

Tripwire

- <u>Defined</u>: A device intended to convert a website visitor into a customer by offering a product with a high *value-to-price ratio*. The tripwire is intended to get customers "in the door" so that they can purchase other products or services from you in the future.

Selected Bibliography

Brunson, Russell. *DotCom Secrets: The Underground Playbook for Growing Your Company Online.* 1st Edition. New York: Morgan James Publishing, 2015.

———. *Expert Secrets: The Underground Playbook for Converting Your Online Visitors into Lifelong Customers.* 1st Edition. Carlsbad, California: Hay House, Inc, 2020.

———. "The Simplest Funnel Business Model." *The Marketing Secrets Show*, Ep. The Simplest Funnel Business Model - Nov 11, 2019

Bevelin, Peter. *Seeking Wisdom: From Darwin to Munger*, 2018.

Cialdini, Robert B. *Influence: The Psychology of Persuasion.* Revised Edition. New York, NY: Collins, 2006.

Cook, Jonathan. *The Perennial Psychology: A Timeless Approach to Understanding Human Nature.* LiveReal LLC, 2020.

Hendricks, Gay. *The Big Leap: Conquer Your Hidden Fear and Take Life to the Next Level.* New York: HarperOne, 2010.

Jorgenson, Eric. *The Almanack Of Naval Ravikant.* Liberty Publishing, 2022.

Kahana, Michael Jacob. *Foundations of Human Memory.* New York: Oxford University Press, 2014.

Kelly, Kevin. "1,000 True Fans." *The Technium* (Blog). https://kk.org/thetechnium/1000-true-fans/.

Munger, Charles T. *Poor Charlie's Almanack: The Wit and Wisdom of Charles T. Munger*, Expanded Third Edition. Edited by Peter D. Kaufman. 3rd edition. Walsworth Publishing Company, 2005.

Sax, David. *The Revenge of Analog: Real Things and Why They Matter.* 1st edition. New York: PublicAffairs, 2016.

Sertillanges, Antonin. *The Intellectual Life: Its Spirit, Conditions, Methods.* Reprint edition. Washington, D.C.: The Catholic University of America Press, 1992.

Settle, Ben. *The 10-Minute Workday.*

———. *BizWorld: How to Create an Irresistible Business Universe Your Customers Love to Buy from and Hate to Leave.* Independently published, 2023.

Sultanic, Alen, and Robert Neckelius. *Automatic Clients*, 2021.

Index

A
Analog
  the power of 99
Analog Book Page 135
Analog Books 138, 170
Analog Knowledge Funnel 128
Analog Knowledge Products 105
Analog Knowledge Tripwire
    124, 127
Analog Monthly Newsletters
    114, 127, 171
  the power of 114
Analog Newsletter Upsell 136
Analog Publishing 118
  vs. digital 118
Antinet 134
Availability Cascade 76
Average Order Value (AOV) 124

B
Backend Product 88, 98
Brodus (Cat) 151
Brunson, Russell 73, 85
Buyer's Heat 124

C
Compounding 114, 161

D
Digital Newsletters 53
Digital Publishing 60, 81

F
Freebie Seekers 175
Frontend Product 88, 98
Funnels 73, 86, 89, 123

G
Greenlamp 173, 223

H
Halbert, Gary 54, 111, 112, 169

I
Imposter Syndrome 66
Incubator 180
Indoctrination 124
  how to 105

K
Kindle Direct Publishing 59
KLT 126
Knowledge
  the first human need 104

L
Luhmann, Niklas 133

M
Monthly Recurring Revenue
    (MRR) 184
Mormons 74, 91

221

N
Neo-Intellectual Life 48, 57
Niches 76

O
One-Time-Only Offer 87

P
Penpreneur 190
Permissionless Leverage 57

R
Recurring Revenue 114, 127
René, Hailey 181

S
Settle, Ben 88, 113

T
Tribes
  of superfans 197
Tripwires 88, 124

U
Upsells 87

W
Write to Freedom 180, 202

Z
Zettelkasten 133

About the Author

Scott P. Scheper (aka, "*The Analog Knowledge Revolutionary*") spends his days reading, writing, and installing notecards in his Antinet.[1] When not writing (with one of his nine Montblanc pens), Scott can be found working with his *Freedom Writers*—a group of "crazies" enrolled in *Write to Freedom*.

When not spearheading the *Analog Knowledge Revolution*, Scott spends time with his best friend, his wife (aka, the "earth angel"). At the time of this writing, Scott is gearing up for the arrival of his first-born son, Fitzgerald Scott Scheper (aka, "Fitzy").

To stay in touch, Scott highly advises that you subscribe to his analog monthly newsletter, *The Scott Scheper Letter*. You can get a thirty-day free trial by visiting **www.ScottScheper.com/Free-Trial**

---

[1] You can learn more about the Antinet here: www.ScottScheper.com/antinet

Greenlamp

Greenlamp is the platform that powers Scott's entire analog knowledge business. It enables him to launch Analog Knowledge Funnels, **analog** books, analog monthly newsletters, and more.

If you would like a free 30-day trial of *Greenlamp*, please visit: **www.Greenlamp.com**